Public Authority
Procurement Strategy

Public Authority Procurement Strategy

Institution of Civil Engineers

Edited by David Hodgkinson

 Thomas Telford

THE INSTITUTION OF
CIVIL ENGINEERS

Published by Thomas Telford Publishing, Thomas Telford Ltd, 1 Heron Quay, London E14 4JD. URL http://www.thomastelford.com

Distributors for Thomas Telford books are
USA: ASCE Press, 1801 Alexander Bell Drive, Reston, VA 20191-4400, USA
Japan: Maruzen Co. Ltd, Book Department, 3–10 Nihonbashi 2-chome, Chuo-ku, Tokyo 103
Australia: DA Books and Journals, 648 Whitehorse Road, Mitcham 3132, Victoria

First published 2001

A catalogue record for this book is available from the British Library

ISBN: 0 7277 3022 3

Typeset by Ian Kingston Editorial Services, Nottingham, UK.
Printed and bound in Great Britain by Hobbs the Printer.

Contents

Acknowledgements

Working Party
David Hodgkinson, Chair and Editor
Elinor Goodchild, secretariat
Harry Potts
Dick Huskinson, Borough Technical Services Officer, Borough, of Chesterfield
Mike Stephens, Kent County Council, Area Manager West Kent
Roger Gardner, Highways and Transportation Services Manager, Essex County Council
William Woolley, Assistant Director (Development and Transport) City of York Council
Brian Rees, Director of Leisure and Technical Services, Christchurch Borough Council
With thanks for contributions from Guy Cottam and Rosemary Beales

Consultees
Association of Consulting Engineers (ACE)
Civil Engineering Contractors Association (CECA)
Construction Industry Research and Information Association (CIRIA)
ICE Industry Practices Committee
The Association of Municipal Engineers (AME)
Office of Government Commerce (OGC)
CSS
Technical Advisers Group – Operations Management and Procurement Committee
Chartered Institution of Public Finance Accountants (CIPFA)
With further thanks to John Jackson, DETR

1 Objectives and reasons for this publication

Local Government exists in order to provide the local community with a range of services which individuals need but cannot provide by themselves. Taken together, Local Government services materially affect the quality of life enjoyed by individuals, the environment and the economic prosperity of the area.

UK Local Government has unique problems:

- Without powers of general competence,[1] Authorities can undertake only those activities that Central Government directs. Whilst some directions are mandatory – with which Authorities must comply – others offer options for Authorities to choose.
- Local Government is not self-financing. A very high proportion of both capital and revenue finance is obtained from Central Government or other funders. So Authorities are beholden to their funders as to how money is spent. Although a high proportion of both capital and revenue finance is sourced by Central Government, Authorities do fund works through capital receipts, for example by sale of assets. Authorities are also responsible for setting their own local taxation levels and are accountable to the local community.
- As never before, Authorities must achieve defined performances and are audited and inspected to ensure that they do.

The current 'Best Value' regime further reinforces the pressure on Authorities to operate effectively and economically. Both value for money and the imperative of continuously improving performance drive Authorities to ensure that the manner in which they procure goods and services is effective and efficient. Much can go wrong in the appointment and supervision of contractors, especially where complex services or construction is entailed.

---

1   Note that the Local Government Act 2000 gives limited powers of general competence in pursuit of well-being. The Act and explanatory notes can be obtained from HMSO (ISBNs 0 10 542 200 2 and 0 10 562 000 9, repsectively).

Best Value demands that procurement strategies be reviewed. Any resultant changes must deliver better value. There is no *one* ideal way to procure services. Each situation is different. However, there are clear methods for choosing the most appropriate (or best) way for any given circumstance, and there is a logical process which should be followed to confirm decisions will indeed deliver the best.

Evolutionary procurement processes are developing. The Egan Report (now subsumed within the 'Movement for Innovation') places a heavy emphasis on quality, client leadership, supply chain management, and research (see `http://www.knowledgeexchange.org.uk`) and development, leading to higher productivity and profit margins. Consequently, competition will be based on a wide range of judgemental factors, not simply price.

Underlying procurement are certain inalienable principles. In the final analysis, competition is the most effective means of securing the required quality of service at lowest cost, but partnership is the foundation of efficiency. Competition must be open and fair. Personal integrity is expected of the individuals involved and is not negotiable. Deviation from the principles of competition, whilst not impossible, must be undertaken with great care and transparency.

The aim of this document is to interpret statutory Best Value requirements and provide a practical guide for Authority Members and staff as to the right way to choose a procurement strategy. This guide focuses on construction and services provided over a period of time rather than purchases of goods or equipment. It is the more complex service contracts that have the highest potential for error and inefficiency. So the following chapters:

- clarify what and how decisions on procurement should be made
- discuss how greater economy may be achievedcConsider issues of probity and integrity
- consider the longer-term consequences of decisions made now
- review legislation and other rules that must be followed
- advise on best practice, including reviews of past performance
- clarify appropriate methods of monitoring contracts.

But above all, the guide is born of practical experience of what works and what can go wrong.

Note that throughout this guide, 'Authority' can be interpreted as any statutory body other than Central Government.

2 How to choose a procurement strategy

Procurement is an expensive process. The potential for waste and error is high. The potential for failing to meet people's expectations is higher still. The process needs to be properly planned and managed. Whilst the Authority is well advised to have a team of trained specialists, an experienced individual should be identified to take responsibility for the management of the procurement process. Whilst continuity of responsibility throughout the process is preferable, any transfer from one individual to another should be clear and fully documented.

The procurement process comprises several stages that are complex and lengthy. The process manager will need to draw on the expertise of others and may benefit from the appointment of advisers. Authorities' key procurement decisions are often made by Members. So the procurement policy and process should be agreed with the appropriate Members and specific stages at which Members' formal decisions will be needed should be identified with them.

Step 1 – Identifying needs

Always begin at the end. Be clear about what the community needs. Visualize and articulate the expected outcome. Decide what is important and what is not. The catastrophic and expensive failures of procurement are almost always the consequence of a lack of clarity of the expected outcome.

Plan the procurement process to meet the required outcome. Whether the subject is a new service, or the continuation of an existing one, the first step is to ensure that the 'investment' will meet the target community's requirements. Various techniques of 'market research' and 'community engagement' are available. This document does not seek to advise on what research techniques to use for particular circumstances. However, a clear and full understanding of who the target community is and what their needs and expectations are is essential. Hearsay, professional judgement and Members' opinions, on their own, are wholly insufficient. Decisions must be informed by proper research.

Step 2 – The brief

The worst procurement failures are often the result of an inadequate (or even the absence of a) brief. The brief is a written description of the completed project or service. It sets out what the expected outcome should be, what role the contractor will play and the constraints and difficulties in delivering the project. Whereas the contract 'specification' will detail the standard of materials and activities that the contractor will be obliged to perform, the brief is the means of communicating the whole expected outcome to all the people involved. The brief will explain:

- the facilities or services to be procured
- how they are to be used in future
- what roles they will play in meeting community need
- how they will fit into their environment
- the further stages of the procurement process.

The brief is like an output specification. It describes the end result, but not just of the procurement itself. The brief clarifies how the intended procurement combines with other activities to help achieve the Authority's overall goals.

The brief should be drafted carefully by the project manager. An 'output' specification could be used as an alternative to a brief for simpler projects. In both cases a clear, unambiguous style and layout helps others to understand. It is essential to consult others on the content of the brief to ensure requirements are accurately and comprehensively set down so as to meet the defined expectations. The following should be consulted:

- those who will use or benefit from the acquisition or service
- those who may suffer any kind of loss or 'disbenefit'
- those who will manage the resultant facility
- those with experience of similar procurements
- Members of the sponsoring Authority
- other Public Authorities or public bodies having responsibilities in the area
- utility companies, especially if their plant may be affected or their products involved
- Residents' Associations
- local Chambers of Commerce or other similar bodies
- contractors with experience of delivering this type of service or facility.

The purpose and timing of the consultation should be stated explicitly. Once responses have been received, and the brief modified appropriately, it should be formally endorsed by the Authority.

Step 3 – Check the facts

The second most frequent cause of problem between clients and contractors are things that existed at the outset but had not been identified. For example, there have been innumerable cases of unforeseen ground conditions, which have led to costly disputes between the parties. So it is imperative that full surveys are undertaken and documented describing the existing situation. These may include:

- topography
- soil and ground conditions
- existing traffic and movement patterns
- the location and state of and buildings or facilities the contractor may be expected to use or may be affected by the contractor's activities
- ambient environmental conditions
- number and locations of people to receive the service or who may be affected by it
- availability of materials
- compatibility with other works.

All this information should be collated and made available to the tenderers for the procurement contract. However, contractors are usually expected to form their own judgement of the information and to collect whatever additional available information they consider to be necessary (this would be a joint exercise in a partnering contract).

Step 4 – Secure the finance

In order to obtain the finance, a business plan should be prepared. Business planning has been ignored too often by Authorities, leading to a lack of proper planning and consequent problems at later stages in the process. Advice on the content and preparation of business plans is available elsewhere. But of particular concern in the procurement process is the preparation of financial forecasts. These forecasts should include:

- the total expenditure on the procurement itself and the timing of when that expenditure will occur
- the costs and incomes (or savings) accruing from the new service or facility and when these can be expected to accrue
- the costs and timing of ongoing maintenance and renewals
- the cost of any advice that will be needed.

For the procurement of a service over a period of time, the business plan should cover the whole period showing individual annual forecasts and allowing for the costs of extending the initial contract or procuring another contractor to continue the service provision at the end of the initial term. The financial implications of future improvements or modifications of the procurement contract should be included in the business plan. Similarly, the financial analysis of a new asset or facility should include not only the first year of operation but also a subsequent year when full operation and full maintenance costs are likely to be experienced.

This range of financial information is likely to be a requirement if the source of finance is from outside the promoting Authority. But a comprehensive business plan should be prepared in any case.

Step 5 – Constraints and rules

Subsequent chapters of this document set out three major sources of constraint or rules:

- EC Directives, generally governing the manner in which all large contracts should be advertised and tenderers selected.
- UK Legislation, covering a range of issues including the use of adjudication to settle disputes and timing of payments.
- Council Financial Regulations, especially the Standing Orders relating to contract procedures that every Authority must have and observe. The detail of these will vary between Authorities.

In addition, Best Value legislation and subsequent guidance requires the observance of certain procedures. The designated procurement manager must become familiar with all of the constraints and rules. Ignorance is no defence.

Step 6 – Risk allocation

Those tendering for a contract need to know the degree of risk they are expected to take. The higher the risk taken, the greater must be the financial provision in case the worst actually happens. Consequently, the higher the risk a contractor assumes, the greater will be the tender value and hence cost born by the client. Whereas careful checking of the facts about the existing circumstance will help to reduce the total risk, there will always be elements of uncertainty outside the control of all the parties to a contract. But everyone needs to know for which risks they are responsible, in order that they can make a suitable financial provision either by adding to the cost of the proposal or by spreading the risk by such means as acquiring insurance.

Even if all possible measures are taken to clarify what outcome is expected, there will always be risk attached to the procurement processes. All likely or possible risks should be identified by the procurement process manager and explicitly assigned to a particular party to the procurement contract. If this is not done, the following may well happen:

- funders will refuse or place high premiums on any finance required
- tender prices will be unexpectedly high
- the total cost of acquiring the service or facility will be unnecessarily high.

The business plan and the contract documents are the mechanisms for allocating risk. Standard contract documents may well be preferred, since contractors and others will be familiar with the risk allocation. Creating unique contract documentation is advisable only in unique circumstances, and then experienced professional advice should be sought.

Step 7 – Type of contract

There is no single best form of contract for all types of procurement. There may well be a best contract for a specific case. Thus the particular characteristics of each procurement should be analysed so as to choose the most suitable form of contract. The key considerations and the availability of standard contracts are set out in other chapters.

Much has been said of the apparent benefits of forming a strong partnership between the Authority as client and a particular contractor. Adversarial behaviour is of benefit to no one. Any form of contract can be managed with competence and integrity by the individuals concerned. The concept of partnering to pool expertise is sound. However, if the practice of partnering leads to the avoidance of competitive tendering and the use of very long-term contracts there may well be undesirable consequences. By definition, partnering is not possible between an Authority and its own DLO; however, the two should work closely together.

Step 8 – Selecting the tenderers

Unless it is imperative to do so, do not use 'open tendering'. Open tendering allows anyone to tender for the provision of a service. Experience confirms that the lowest price received is likely to be from inexperienced contractors. Problems are likely to result. The Authority should initially seek expressions of interest from experienced contractors. Applicants should then be vetted on the basis of technical expertise to undertake the service and financial standing. Assessments of both factors should be fair and be based on current information. This exercise uses the resources of both potential contractors and the Authority. If practicable, 'standing lists' of potential, suitable contractors should be maintained for a period of time rather than repeat the exercise for every proposed contract. It is still advisable to check the current financial standing of a contractor immediately before entering into a new contract. The DETR's construction line may assist in the process (see `http://www.constructionline.co.uk`).

Step 9 – Evaluation

Until recently, Authorities chose contractors invariably on the basis of the lowest tender price. The specification in the contract was relied upon to dictate the quality of the service delivered. The Authority's Standing Orders should be reviewed so that tenders can be evaluated on other factors as well as price. These additional considerations must be explicit, relevant and fair (see Chapter 12).

The tender evaluation system should be available to potential tenderers at the outset. Indeed, EC Directives require that the evaluation factors be stated in the initial Notice inviting tenderers to apply to be on the 'select list'. If a combination of, say, price, quality, time and so on is to be used for tender evaluation, then the formula that allocates weights to these factors should be devised and tested on the range of tender returns that may be received. Qualitative analysis should be based on predetermined factors. In essence, even the tenderer should be able to evaluate the tender with the same resultant 'score' as the client would calculate.

You should not evaluate tenders by yourself, except where lowest price is the only consideration. Where qualitative factors are included, a panel of at least three experienced persons should be involved. The recommendation of the panel may have to be referred to a Committee of Members of the Authority for their endorsement.

Step 10 – Monitoring the contract

Contractors will apply their expertise to the contract. There are sound reasons why the client Authority should employ its own experts to monitor the progress of the Contractor:

- Mistakes can be made. Whilst the Contractor is responsible for his or her errors, resultant problems could be avoided if the Contractor were advised of an error at an early stage.
- Payment of the Contractor is likely to be based on his achievements. The amount due to the Contractor should be verified independently.
- Best Value demands continuous improvements. How these are achieved and the consequent sharing of financial benefits must be agreed between the contractor and client.

- Each contract is part of a complex of service provision. Each contract needs to be coordinated with other activities to ensure that the Authority can achieve Best Value for service provision as a whole.

Both the Authority and the Contractor should designate individuals to be the key point of contact between the two bodies. The Authority is well advised to select an experienced person. There should be a mechanism for reporting the progress of the Contractor to a Committee of the Authority, from time to time.

Difference of opinion or even disputes may arise between the Contractor and the Authority. The Contract itself should set out the means of resolving these. UK Legislation requires that adjudication be available. Any dispute, unless resolved at an early stage, is likely to be costly and disruptive to the Authority (see Chapter 17).

Step 11 – Reviewing the process

Procurement is a lengthy and complex process. There is always room for improvement. The Authority should undertake reviews of:

- whether the contract has met the original service objectives
- whether people's needs and expectations have changed such that the contract should be modified
- whether the procurement process itself could be improved
- how external factors, such as legislation and standard contracts, have changed.

Reviews should be pre-planned and the outcome reported to appropriate Members of the Authority.

Some final guidance

Seek expert advice, knowing what questions you require answered. Advice may be needed to:

- help the promoting Authority to identify precisely what is needed
- 'design' the outcome
- prepare the business plan and find the finance
- confirm the legal constraints and procedures
- supervise, monitor and audit the process
- review whether the resultant service fully meets people's needs.

But above all, understand and plan the procurement process.

3 Best Value requirements

What is Best Value?

The Government requires Authorities to demonstrate Best Value in all their activities. The prime aim is to establish a culture of continuous improvement in the performance of every Authority. However, the Government seeks an initial 'step change' in performance. There are many different ways in which Best Value is being addressed around the country. Indeed, one of the strengths of Best Value is that it allows some flexibility in its application. Central, of course, are the economy and the effectiveness and efficiency of service provision and its procurement. To these three Es should be added equity and environment. Best Value was introduced through a number of pilot projects, which were intended to inform its full implementation. In practice, the pilots had insufficient time to yield fully beneficial results before the Government enacted new regulations. With the new legislation came the demise of Compulsory Competitive Tendering (CCT). The government has, however, stressed that competition should form an integral part of any Authority procurement strategy.

The Local Government Act 1999 sets out the general duty of Best Value with effect from 1 April 2000. From this date the Audit Commission became responsible for a new Best Value inspection role. There will be periodic inspections of Authorities' Best Value reviews and tests of service improvements. All Authorities are required to set out their programme of reviews in a Best Value Performance Plan, such that all their activities and services are reviewed within five years. There is a legal requirement for Authorities to revise and publish their Best Value Performance Plan by 31 March each year.

Why is Best Value different?

Best Value is underpinned by the four Cs:

- Challenge
- Consult
- Compare
- Compete

These four combined should serve to identify how continuous improvement is to be achieved. When applied to any service, they provide a far more rigorous and comprehensive analysis of service provision.

Best Value requires Authorities to go back to basic principles and to fundamentally **challenge** not just for whom and how a service should be provided but whether it should be provided at all. In particular, procurement mechanisms should be fundamentally re-examined.

Consultation with customers is key. It is the customer who should inform the procurer what service is required, and equally how the service should be carried out. This applies not only to ongoing services but also to one-off works. For example, customer consultation can inform the way a highway improvement contract is carried out so as to minimize disruption. The suppliers of goods and services should be consulted on available materials, methods and likely costs.

An authority should ensure that it has chosen the best procurement process by **comparing** itself with other organizations that provide similar services, including those in the private and voluntary sectors. This comparison process should be with the best providers of the same or similar services in both the public and private sectors.

A rigorous comparison regime can provide clear benchmark indicators against which to judge the Authority's performance. But, in the final analysis, the best judge is **competition**.

Procurement of goods and services under Best Value

An Authority should establish first whether it has a statutory duty to provide a service or whether, although it has the power, the decision to provide it is discretionary. Authorities may choose to go far beyond their statutory duty in the provision of a given service, but must establish their reasons. Reasons include satisfying the expressed wishes of their customers, established through structured consultation. Proper consultation should identify what customers think of the service now and what improvements are needed. Consultation should be both qualitative and quantitative, or, in other words, relate to both feeling and fact. One of the fundamental differences between Best Value and CCT is that the former not only allows, but also actively encourages, local variation in services when these are justified by customer requirements. The qualitative element expected of a service should be reflected in the subsequent procurement requirements. Quality issues will inevitably involve service process requirements rather than just outputs. However, care must be taken in not being too prescriptive, as this may constrain effective competition and stifle innovation.

Government has reaffirmed that Strategic Partnerships are essential to the procurement process. These are fundamentally different from the traditional approaches to contracting; they are quality driven and value added. Best Value demands that these two latter elements are evaluated and demonstrable.

A single approach to procurement of all services is unlikely to meet criteria of effectiveness and efficiency. The Government recognizes that Authority services are extremely diverse. It is therefore logical that the methods of procurement of those services are themselves diverse if they are to meet with the requirements of Best Value.

> *... deliver services to clear standards – covering both cost and quality – by the most effective, economic and efficient means available.*

Competition is encouraged and alternative providers should be investigated so as to clarify what options are available to deliver a service. If in-house provision is an option, it should be tested through a competitive process, particularly if the service has previously been provided in-house. If a full competitive process is not pursued, there will need to be a rigorous method of establishing the cost of in-house service provision so as to compare with what others could provide.

The new approach which the public sector is being encouraged to adopt can be delivered in various ways:

- joint ventures
- strategic contracts
- franchise arrangements
- companies in partnership
- community trusts

or a combination of these. But you should check for any statutory constraints.

Whatever form of procurement is used, Best Value requires that it must allow for ongoing performance monitoring. The procurement plan for a particular service should therefore take into account not only the performance of the provider in terms of both process and outcome, but also how that performance will be measured. A useful guide on developing and using performance indicators is provided by the Audit Commission in their publication, *A Measure of Success* (February 1999).

A Measure of Success *states that performance indicators adopted by Authorities should:*

- *focus attention on what kind of service is needed and to make it clear – to the council, their staff and the public – what level of service is expected*
- *help managers to direct effort to priorities*
- *help councils to know when they need to adjust services and resources*
- *provide a route for public involvement in planning services*
- *develop a climate of continuous service improvement*
- *put local standards in a national context*
- *help the council to hold contractors to account for performance.*

Help the public to see whether services are being delivered efficiently and effectively, and so hold the council to account.

Performance management can be incorporated into procurement and subsequent service provision in three layers:

- national context
- accountability
- continuous service improvement.

The whole of the decision-making process, both in initial procurement and subsequent monitoring of performance, should be easily audited. Often known as an 'audit trail', the decisions and reasons for them should be recorded systematically to enable subsequent review. The chosen procurement process should demonstrably conform to the primary tests of Best Value, rather than specific detailed requirements.

Benefits of Best Value

Best Value moves away from 'lowest price' as the sole determinant. It allows the introduction of quality, value and other relevant criteria. It is undoubtedly true that Best Value when properly applied is more onerous than CCT in the procurement of services, but Authorities who rise to the challenge will derive considerable benefits.

In summary these benefits are:

- challenges both the need and the way services are provided
- links services to customer requirements
- allows flexibility in approach (unlike CCT)
- encourages quality as an elementary consideration
- allows local factors to be taken into account
- includes all services

- gives the opportunity to demonstrate value for money (through benchmarking, PIs and competition)
- provides for ongoing monitoring and review to inform the management process.

Clearly Authorities have a duty to fundamentally review the way in which they procure works and services. The evidence of the review process should be collated so as to demonstrate its thoroughness to the Best Value Inspectorate.

4 EC Procurement Directives

Introduction

Since 1993, all major Authority Contracts for goods, services or building works are covered by EC Directives on Public Procurement, now transposed into UK Law through regulations as the 'Public Supply Services Contracts Regulations 1993'. (The Services Regulations). Anyone in Local Government involved in awarding contracts (or bidding for contracts) will therefore need to know what these Regulations require.

European Directives do not require Councils to contract externally. If, however, they do so, through competitive tendering, these are the rules that must be followed. However, they apply only if a specified contract value threshold is exceeded.

The EC Rules are obligatory and failure to comply with them is a breach of the law. There is pressure to change the wording in the Directive so as to allow the lowest priced bid to be rejected if there is adequate justification. The underlying principle is that any Public Procurement System should be seen to be fair to all parties, including the taxpayers.

The detailed EC procedures start at the point in which the contract is to be advertised, and are completed once the contract has been awarded.

Key questions

All Authority Contracts over the specified relevant threshold will be covered by one or other of the Directives. For each procurement, there are three key questions:

- whether the contract is governed by the Works, Supplies or Services Regulations
- whether the contract falls into any of the exempt categories
- whether the value of the contract falls above the threshold.

Thresholds

The regulations do not apply to contracts with an estimated value (net of VAT) of less than:

- for works contracts: €5,358,153
- for supply contracts: €214,326
- for service contracts: €214,326, with certain exceptions, notably part B services where the threshold is reduced to €200,000.

NB The value of sterling equivalent to the euro changes every two years. The value effective from 1 January 2000 to 31 December 2001 is €1.4837 to £1.00.

Definitions of contract types

'Works Contracts' are those covering activities included in a schedule set out in the Regulations within the broad headings of:

- general buildings and civil engineering and demolition work
- construction of residential and non-residential flats, office blocks, hospitals and other buildings
- civil engineering in relation to construction of roads, bridges and railways
- installation of fixtures and fittings such as gas, heating, electrical services
- building, finishings work, including painting, plastering, joinery and tiling.

'Supply contracts' include the purchasing or hiring of goods by a contracting Authority, including any siting or installation of these goods. However, where the contract also includes the provision of a service, the Supply Regulations will apply only if the cost of the goods (and any siting or installation of them) is greater than the value attributable to the services.

'Service Contracts' are any contracts in writing and involving payments between a service provider and a client Authority, other than:

- contracts covered by the supply or Works Regulations
- contracts for the buying or renting of land, existing buildings, or other fixed property
- contracts for telephones, telex, paging and satellite services
- contracts for financial services in connection with securities, financial instruments and central banking
- contracts for arbitration and conciliation services
- employment contracts
- research and development service contracts.

Aggregation

The general principle of Aggregation is that contracts must not be divided or arranged simply to ensure that they fall below the respective value threshold.

Similar contracts must be added together for the purpose of the thresholds. However, these rules need not apply to discrete operational units with delegated budgets and with a delegated power to purchase. Contracts entered into for goods or services which are not for the operational unit's sole use will not, however, be exempt from aggregation.

For Supply Contracts, the relevant value will be the total value of the contract. Where the contract is for the hire of goods for an indefinite period, the value to be calculated is the monthly hire sum multiplied by 48.

Prior Indicative Notice

The following Prior Indicative Notices are required:

- *Works*. Authorities must send to the official journal (OJEC) a notice in the prescribed form as soon as possible after the decision approving the planning of the work or works.
- *Services*. Authorities must publish an annual notice in the OJEC at the start of the financial year if they estimate that the total value of contracts they will award in that year in any one priority services category is above a threshold €750,000.
- *Supplies*. There is no legislation in force at present requiring Authorities to send Prior Indicative Notices.

Contract procedures

The procedures to be followed by an Authority must comply with the respective Authority's Standing Orders, but the EC Directives take precedent.

Legal sanctions

EC legislation provides legal remedies against Councils where the specified procedures are not followed. The UK courts are empowered to grant remedies to third parties who have an interest in the tendering process, whether invited to tender or not.

An aggrieved contractor's or supplier's claim must be for loss or damage suffered as a result of an Authority's actions (which must be proved), and before bringing a claim, he or she must inform the Authority of the complaint and the intention to take court proceedings. The proceedings must be brought within three months of the date when grounds for complaint first arose (Works Regulations Part vii, Supply Regulations Part vii, Services Regulations Part vii).

If a claim is successful, the Court may order:

- *Suspension*: By interim order suspend the procedures leading to the award of the contract or suspend the implementation of any decision or action by the contracting Authority.
- *Set aside*: Order the setting aside of a decision, action, order the Contracting Authority to amend any document (including the removal of discriminatory technical, economic or financial specifications).
- *Award damages*: Award damages to a Contractor or Supplier who has suffered loss or damage as a result of a breach of the Regulations.
- *Set aside and award damages*: The Court may set aside the decision and award damages. If the contract in question has already been entered into, the Court has only the power to award damages.

Remedies Directive Article 3

Provisions also exist which enable the European Commission itself to take action against an Authority via Government. If the Commission considers that a clear infringement of a contract award procedure has taken place, it can request its correction.

The right of complaint to the Commission by a Contractor/Supplier is not altered by the direct access to the courts described above. The complainant's identity may also be kept confidential.

Authorities need to remain aware that in addition to the power of the Commission and remedies available to aggrieved Contractors/Suppliers, other more general controls on their activities exist, including:

- judicial review
- claims in tort (civil wrong) in respect of failure to comply with statutory duties
- complaints to the Ombudsman
- challenges by District Auditors.

5 Council financial regulations

The need for Standing Orders

Without exception, all Authorities have their own Standing Orders (SO) designed to ensure probity in the letting of contracts, to provide protection against any false accusations of corruption and to ensure that no influences are exercised by vested interests. In essence the Authority must demonstrate integrity and transparency throughout the processes. SO anticipate fair and open competition and are intended to achieve an effective and efficient contract administration process.

Well drafted SO need to address all relevant matters. Authorities will need to review their SO in light of Best Value requirements. DETR guidance on governance regulations refer to the expectation of CIPFA producing model financial regulations (including SO).[1] Indeed, SO should be regularly updated to reflect changes within the Authority itself, from new legislation or from amendments to the nationally accepted contract conditions that traditionally form the basis of most major contracts. SO should be written in such a way that they do not preclude innovative practices such as negotiated contracts, partnership contracts, DBFO contracts or the need to seek continuous improvement in Term Contracts. It is difficult to draft SO to cope with every contract eventuality. SO benefit from ongoing and regular review, but specific situations can be resolved by 'waiving' SO and obtaining specific direction from the Authority.

The essential review

In its review the Authority should consider the following significant issues.

Simplicity and understanding

SO will often be written in a semi-legal style; nevertheless, they must be understood by all officers involved in procurement. SO may be bound into a document that covers everything from the rules of debate at Council meetings to the claiming of councillors' allowances. The size of the whole

---

1 CIPFA review of the Code of Practice on Local Authority accounting in the UK can be found on the CIPFA website at http://www.cipfa.org.uk.

document may limit its issue to senior managers only; however, the core SO should be distributed to all the staff involved in procurement contracts.

If the Authority produces a contracts procurement handbook, it should include the relevant council SO relating to purchasing and contracts. The handbook must be available to all staff involved in procurement. The SO need to be readily understandable and need to be completely integrated into any other 'departmental' contracts' procedures such as quality assurance schemes. The achievement of unified documentation should be the result of coordination between financial, legal and procurement officers. All Authority officers should be made fully aware of the standards of integrity expected in public service.

Modern management

In recent years, the increased use of quality management systems has seen the widespread use of processes such as decision-making models, procedure flowcharts and action checklists. Such systems, and indeed the whole concept of quality assurance systems, are to be encouraged. However, there is little point in having a file of standing orders that are separate and remote from the operational procurement guidelines. Authorities are strongly advised to produce their SO as one of an integrated family of documents.

It is of paramount importance that standing orders are complied with. Non-compliance should be a disciplinary offence. Any staff responsible for procurement should be taught the practices enumerated in the document.

Pre-tender and tender procedures

SO and procurement handbooks need to be consistent. Instructions must include arrangements for administering 'standing lists', approved contractors, selection of contractors, pre-qualification and tender evaluation, including quality and other relevant considerations.

Procedures may vary depending on the estimated financial value of an intended contract. SO on evaluation of the project should be undertaken before seeking tenders. The anticipated capital costs and the revenue budget consequences should be estimated. For any sizeable project the principles of whole life costing (see Chapter 10) should be applied. SO set out the rules for various means of procurement (for example open tender, negotiated contract, in-house or partnering), but do not usually indicate which is the preferred choice.

Flowcharts illustrating such alternatives can be useful in explaining the processes adopted by an Authority, and a simplified example is shown in Figure 5.1.

Opening and acceptance

Most SO will cover comprehensively the process of opening sealed tenders and should be designed to ensure that no single person or group can be

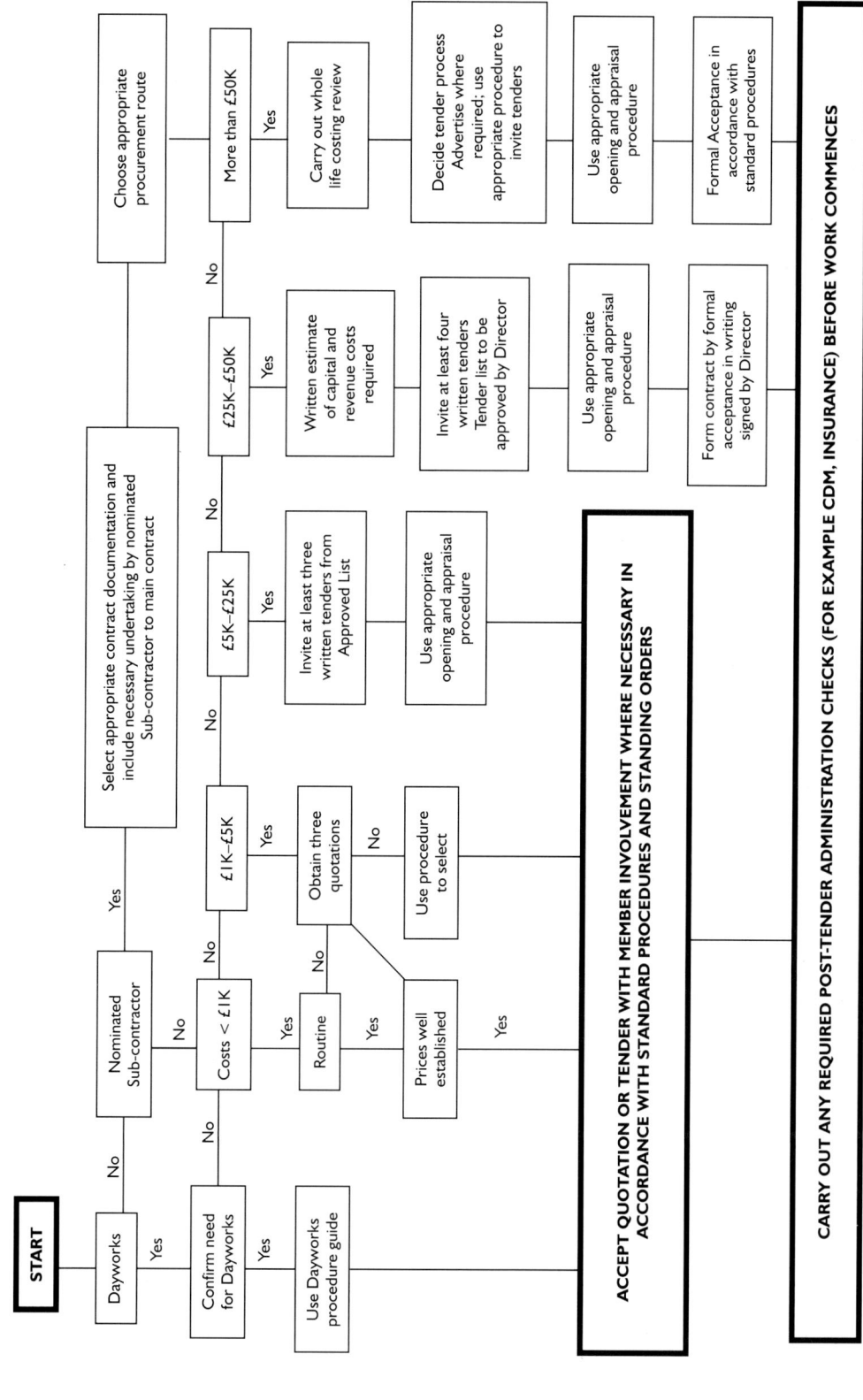

Figure 5.1 Flowchart example – conventional procurement routes. Simplified guide to contract procedures and standing orders.

falsely accused of collusion with any of the tenderers. Clear procedures should be in place for dealing with late tenders received both before and after the opening. Similarly, whilst SO generally require the envelope to bear no indication of the sender, particular procedures should be drafted to allow for outer wrappers such as Registered mail or courier delivery, where the sender's identity may be visible. Tenderers will have incurred preparation costs. Unless there is evidence to the contrary, tenders should be accepted as bona fide. The Authority's underlying aim is to achieve fair competition.

To quote the Salmon Report:

Some public sector bodies will not, under any circumstances, accept franked envelopes or late tenders but others now do accept them. The rigid adherence to the laid down rules may avoid bad practices occurring but it may lead to a loss to the organisation if the later tender or franked envelope is not accepted.

Appendix 17 of Salmon Report as quoted in Financial Information Service, Volume 7 – Procurement, *published by CIPFA.*

SO should allow the earliest possible award of the contract. The successful tenderer will need to programme his or her resources and begin the process of ordering materials. Unsuccessful tenderers will need to know their situation as they tender for other work. SO that require a lengthy process of committee or council approval should be reviewed to see if such a procedure is really needed.

Negotiated contracts

SO should clarify the procedures for negotiated contracts, which may take various forms. Some Authorities require at least two senior officers to be present during contract negotiations, and such a rule is strongly endorsed. The award of negotiated contracts would normally require a more comprehensive approval mechanism than for conventional competitive tenders. It is good practice for Authorities to publish, in advance, their intention to negotiate contracts over £100,000 or 13 weeks in length. The formal notice should give reasons and the name of the proposed negotiation partner. The notice should be placed in local papers and appropriate trade journals, in addition to the *London Gazette.*

The final approval for placing negotiated contracts still rests with the Authority's Council. All preliminary documentation should be available for inspection, both at the time that the Council makes its decision and for any subsequent audit or inspection.

Use of IT

The Government is advocating the use of 'E-procurement' and has set its own departments a time-scale for complete implementation. Authorities should review their position.

'E-procurement' is not limited to email transmission, but includes all varieties of electronic rather than paper communications. Contract documents can be produced on CD, enabling recipients to transmit and print copies as necessary. Notices seeking tenderers can be made available on the Web. Provided the necessary security procedures are in place, tenders can be transmitted to the Authority by email. The potential for efficiency savings is considerable. SO will need to allow for the use of IT in all stages of the process, but with specified safeguards.

Efficiency versus bureaucracy

In carrying out reviews of SO, the balance between an emphasis on probity and the need to avoid unnecessary bureaucracy should be weighed carefully. Onerous tender or contract conditions will involve all tenderers in extra costs that may not be cost-effective to the Authority.

Other considerations

You should reconsider the following:

- Liquidated Damages

  The purpose of Liquidated Damages is to protect the Authority from real financial loss if the contractor fails to complete a project or specified activity to the required time-scale. If the contract includes Liquidated Damages, and the contract completion is delayed, there is *prima facie* liability on the contractor. There can be no enquiry into the actual loss suffered. However, the contractor may have a defence to the claim by proving that the agreed sum is a penalty, rather than an actual loss experienced by the Authority.

  Whether Liquidated Damages are appropriate for any given contract is a fundamental question; however, any Liquidated Damage figure must be a genuine pre-estimate of the likely damage to be suffered by the Authority and not in any way simply a penalty. The way in which the sum was calculated must be based on clear evidence and be open to scrutiny.

- Bonds

  Most Authorities require a bond to be in place for contracts above a certain specified sum. In determining both the contract and bond values, it should be remembered that bonds cost money, and this will be reflected in the tender price. Each Authority should review the need for a bond. The prime reason for requiring a bond is to cover potential additional cost to the Authority should the chosen contractor fail to complete the contract. Such failure could result from liquidation of the contractor or a significant failure to complete the works leading to the expulsion of the contractor. (A bond on a contract could typically cost 2% of the bond value or more in the case of less secure contractors.)

A sufficiently rigorous pre-tender evaluation of prospective tenderers may obviate the need for a performance bond. Government departments do not normally employ bonds, but instead rely upon effective pre-qualification and selective procedures. This process can be assisted by the use of systems such as the Contractor Management Information System (CMIS) (now Constructionline). However, Constructionline has yet to demonstrate that it is free of significant problems. The concept of a database of proven providers is sound, but it must be managed to a standard at least as high as that of the procurement system itself. The DETR advises that bonds should be conditional, not on-demand, and only employed on the basis of a case by case assessment of the risks associated with each contract. Authorities should take due account of the fact that a bond can adversely affect the competition for the contract. Before asking for a bond, consideration should be given whether the benefits of improved competition and value for money which might be obtained by not requiring a bond, outweigh any risk. As an alternative to a bond, the Authority may seek a written guarantee from the parent company of the contractor (where the named contractor is part of a larger organization).

An Authority decided to construct a new swimming pool. The operation of the pool would have an element of ongoing subsidy. The maximum losses the Authority would suffer from late project completion would be the cost of any staff appointed to operate the pool, less the ongoing subsidy. It was decided that the net loss would be negligible. Liquidated Damages were omitted from the contract.

- Insurance
  Works contracts will normally require contractors to demonstrate that they have adequate public liability insurance (typically £2m to £10m for any one occasion but obviously more on higher risk contracts). Once again this can involve the contractor in extra costs and may prove difficult to obtain. Specialist advice should be obtained by your Authority to ensure that the burden on the contractor is not more onerous than really needed. 'Excesses' can be large and should be checked.

  Consultants employed by a Council should also be required to demonstrate that they have adequate professional indemnity and that it will be maintained for as long as the consultant has any liability for the works or services provided. This should be checked before each engagement.

Tender lists
The overall aim of the tender procedure should be to achieve the desired works or services to the quality required and at a fair (not necessarily the

cheapest) price. In the short term, very large tender lists will discourage contractors from submitting serious bids. In the long term, the costs to contractors of tendering exercises involving many firms will increase the administration costs within the industry as a whole. Large tender lists do not therefore have the support of trade and contracting associations, and are not in the Authority's interests. SO need to reflect this concern by limiting the maximum number of individuals invited to tender. There should be some flexibility to allow inclusion of both quality contractors who are known to be competitive and other contractors who are less well known or who have not previously tendered for services to your Authority.

The use of 'select lists' is very useful in this respect. 'Select lists' are drawn up and reviewed at preset time intervals (say 3 to 5 years). Contractors are then drawn by rotation from the list for each new tender opportunity. The Authority may choose to use a centralized service such as the Constructionline database of contractors managed by the DETR.

Peter Gershon suggested in his report to HM Treasury that procurement strategies need to recognize the total costs likely to be incurred by the industry. He found that:

> *Tendering to Government is burdensome and costly to suppliers. Inputs from industry indicated that bidding for Government contracts is typically 10–50% more costly than bidding for comparable projects in the private sector with the key drivers of these cost burdens being the greater level of detail required and more extended time scales.*

Gershon, P. Review of Civil Procurement in Central Government, HM Treasury, April 1999.

Your Authority should recognize the costs of tendering, which will inevitably be recovered by contractors from their clients. SO should seek to minimize costs regardless of the parties involved.

Procurement costs

The cost of the procurement process, sometimes known as transaction costs, can be significant. Indeed, the value of savings from competitive tender exercises can be more than offset by the administrative cost of the tender process itself. This effect is likely to prevail in comparatively low value procurement. SO should allow the use of quotations as opposed to formal tenders. Similarly, when it comes to buying low-cost goods or services, the cost of processing orders and accounts should be calculated. Payment methods should be devised to minimize these costs. Officers involved in procurement should be fully aware of typical costs for each element of the quotation, ordering, tendering, certification and accounting process, so that informed decisions can be made on the most effective procurement path. SO should allow for such cost-beneficial decisions to take place.

6 Term Contracts

For the purposes of this document, a 'Term Contract' is a contract where the contract period (term) is specified, including possible extension facility; where the work or service is also specified; but where the Client, frequently, is unable to specify, at tender stage, the quantity of the work or the extent of the service required. For example, a Term Contract for housing responsive maintenance may require individual unit rates in fine detail, in addition to collective rates, but the only guide to quantities given to the tenderers may be the value and pattern of repairs over a previous period, with no guarantee that this is representative of the future.

The Term Contract can be utilized on a range of works or services: maintenance and minor works (building/civil engineering); specialist building services (lifts, air conditioning, telecoms and so on); contract energy management; financial services; refuse collection; sport and leisure management; and many others.

The contract period (term) will vary with the type of work or service provided. For contract energy management, which frequently involves the contractor in heavy 'up-front' investment, a contract period of 15 years is not unusual. A maintenance and minor works contract, on the other hand, is likely to be only three or four years in length (See Chapter 11).

There are many procurement options, and variations, in use by different organizations. The seven most common options are identified below, together with the benefits and disbenefits of each.

In-house Client, in-house Direct Labour/Direct Service Organization

This is the traditional method of procurement operated by the majority of Authorities prior to the introduction of Compulsory Competitive Tendering (CCT), and by far the most common during the CCT regime. The introduction of CCT led to the creation of separate Client and Contractor roles within Authorities and, with them, confrontation and layers of unnecessary administration. More positively, it also led to the discipline of trading accounts.

Benefits	Disbenefits
• Familiar system	• All risks remain with the Authority
• In-house facilities available to deal with civil emergencies	• All losses are sustained by the Authority
• Any 'profits' returned to Authority	• DLO/DSO skills and capacity may restrict innovation and flexibility
• Local accountability for Contractor	• Danger of introspection
• Client/Contractor team working	• Less flexibility to deal with fluctuating workloads
• Potential for developing a whole service approach	• No process innovation for Client or Contractor
	• Potential conflict between service units

In-house Client and Client Agent, external Contractor

This is possibly the second most common method of procurement for Term Contracts and one which has been in use for many years in some Authorities (pre-dating CCT).

Benefits	Disbenefits
• Familiar system	• Public service ethos at point of service delivery must be learnt
• Client/Client Agent relationship ensures comprehensive brief and contract documentation	• Initial supervision may be required
• Greater Client control	• Facility for front end loading of costs by Contractor
• Service standards not sacrificed to Contractor's special expertise	• No process innovation for Client/Client Agent
• Established procedures; industry familiar	
• Risks shared in accordance with contract	

In-house Client, external Client Agent, external Contractor

This is an option favoured by smaller Authorities that lack in-house expertise for tender preparation and contract management.

Benefits	Disbenefits
• No in-house technical skills needed	• Lack of Client control
• Industry is familiar with the procedure	• Service details defined by others
	• Little incentive to control costs
	• Learning curve for Client Agent
	• Less accountability for budgetary control
	• Public service ethos at point of delivery must be learnt
	• Risk/benefit balance determined by third party

In-house Client, external 'packaged service' provider

This is another option favoured by smaller Authorities and also by Housing Associations and other quangos. It is an easy option.

Benefits	Disbenefits
● No need for Client skills	● Contractor determines service
● No in-house technical skills required	● No Client quality control
● Contractor submits complete service proposal	● Client variations can be costly
	● Inflexible service
● Costs are known in advance – reduced cost overruns	● Service limited by Contractor skills

Full-scale privatization with asset transfer

Favoured by some Authorities that are confident in their ideology and also by others in response to over-restrictive controls (especially on capital expenditure) from Central Government. Often the last resort option.

Benefits	Disbenefits
● Transfers both risk and responsibility to the private sector	● Abrogation of political responsibility
	● Client ceases to be the Client
● Permits greatly reduced staffing levels in-house	● 'Customers' pay the price of privatization
● Access to private sector finance without Government controls	● Costs may be transferred to the welfare system
● Freedom in the market-place	● Can lead to ghettoization in the housing service
● Potential for developing whole service approach	● Social aspects of service inevitably sacrificed to market forces

Hybrid arrangement: DLO/DSO plus Partnership with specialist or top-up Suppliers or Contractors

This is theoretically the best of both worlds, using the specialist skills of the private sector plus its flexibility to enhance a core in-house service. This option is favoured by professionals and may well emerge as the most common outcome of Best Value service reviews.

Benefits	Disbenefits
● In-house Client and Client Agent skills maintain service levels	
● In-house Contractor facility to respond to emergencies	
● Public service ethos at point of delivery	
● Greater flexibility to meet workload peaks	
● Service not constrained by DLO/DSO skills and capacity	
● Teamwork develops over time	

In-house Client/Client Agent with partnering with a series of external Contractors and/or Suppliers plus in-house Contractor

This option has existed, often unofficially, for many years, particularly in those work areas where multi-discipline works or supplies are required at short notice, for example responsive corporate property repairs and maintenance. This option mirrors very closely what happens in the private sector.

Benefits	Disbenefits
● Permits very responsive service provision	● Danger of 'cosy' relationships developing between Client Agent and Contractors
● Total flexibility to meet workload peaks	
● Service not constrained by skill or capacity of any one organization	
● In-house Contractor facility to respond to emergencies	
● External Contractors/Suppliers develop loyalty to Client	

Many of the options for procurement of technical services through the medium of Term Contracts are similar to those for Single Activity contracts (considered in the next chapters). With all procurement it is important that the procedure has, at its heart, a form of contract that is familiar to all parties. Bespoke contract forms, favoured by 'packaged service' providers, are a recipe for added cost, confusion and confrontation. **Whatever contract form is chosen, a clear and unambiguous Client brief is vital to a successful procurement.** It is also important that the allocation of risk is clearly defined in the partnering contract, as it is in all of the standard contract forms, and that, where risk is shared, the basis of the sharing is also absolutely clear.

Future possibilities – how to develop the concept

Variations on the above options are available depending on the field of work or service under consideration. One particularly interesting option which tends to be found in the energy field is the Capital Turnkey Project allied to an extended operation and maintenance contract, which allows future income streams to accrue to the Contractor in return for a reduced capital payment. This option is a halfway house toward a Private Finance Initiative (PFI) option, but without the strings of Government regulation attached.

Another variation, which is finding favour, particularly in service contracts, is the Output Specification Contract. This option requires a highly competent Client/Client Agent to formulate the specification and to assess the tenders. It does, however, overcome many of the disbenefits associated with the 'packaged service' option and leaves Contractors free to manage their resources in the most effective manner.

Energy management

A number of local authorities have replaced obsolete boiler plants at leisure centres and other buildings with Combined Heat and Power units, financed, maintained and operated by the plant supplier. Under the arrangement, the supplier installs and maintains the CHP unit throughout its life. Payment to the supplier is based on a sum per kWh of useful electricity supplied to the Client Authority within certain defined hours each day. Thus it is in the interests of both the authority and the supplier to ensure that the plant is of optimum size, has optimum availability (hours run), and is maintained and operated at optimum efficiency. It also meets the high cost of major plant replacement without recourse to the public purse.

---

7 Single Activity contracts

'Single Activity' procurement refers to the design and provision of a capital asset. This could be anything that comes within the purview of the Municipal Technical Services Officer: a road scheme, sewer scheme, factory unit, office building, car park, children's play area and so on.

Various distinct procurement strategies have been identified for the Single Activity contract. The strategies, together with the benefits and disbenefits of each, are set out below.

In-house Client and Designer, external Contractor by price contract

This is the traditional method of acquiring capital assets for all but the smallest Authority. As with other procurement strategies, this is not mutually exclusive and frequently will be restricted to 'normal' assets. Specialist activities may be acquired differently.

Benefits	Disbenefits
● No learning curve for the design team (hence better value)	● More detailed involvement of both Client and Planning staff at early stages can lead to longer lead times
● Designer acts as Client Agent to refine brief (in-house knowledge)	● Front end loading of design resources (costs)
● More certainty of out-turn costs	● Less flexibility to deal with fluctuating workloads
● Design not constrained by external factors	● No risk/benefit sharing of time/cost of project out-turn
● Greater Client control	
● Functionality not sacrificed to 'design concepts' and the outcome is purpose-built	● Propensity for 'Confrontational Procurement'
● More regard to whole life costing, hence value for money	● Close supervision of the construction process may be required
● Energy-efficient design solutions receive appropriate weightings (holistic design)	● Change is expensive
● Ease of maintenance considered early in the design process	
● Tried and tested, well-established procedures, industry familiar	

In-house Client and Designer, in-house DLO constructs by fixed price tender

This is an option that may not be open to many Authorities who either do not have a DLO or who keep only a small core DLO function to respond to emergencies.

Benefits	Disbenefits
• All of the benefits of the first procurement option plus:	• All of the disbenefits of the first procurement option plus:
• No profit motive (all profits returned to the Authority)	• All risk remains with Authority
• Local accountability for 'contractor'	• Remedial works at Authority's expense
• Develop team working over a series of projects	• DLO capacity restricts flexibility of programmes
	• All losses are sustained by the Authority

In-house Client/Client Agent, external Designer, external Contractor by price tender

This is an option favoured either to deal with peak workloads or for specialist activity contracts. It may not be available for the very smallest of Authorities that do not have an expert Client Agent facility.

Benefits	Disbenefits
• Client Agent to prepare/refine brief	• More highly developed Client brief is necessary
• Reasonable certainty of out-turn costs	• Designers have no long-term involvement with the project
• Design specialisms can be introduced	• No risk/benefit sharing of time/costs
• Outcome is purpose-built – functionality	• Possibility of additional confrontation is introduced (more parties involved)
• Life cycle criteria (for example energy efficiency, maintainability of elements) can be specified	
• Flexibility to cover fluctuations in design workload	

In-house Client, external Client Agent/Designer, external Contractor by fixed price tender

This is an option favoured by small Authorities which lack the technical expertise to perform the 'expert Client Agent' function.

Benefits	Disbenefits
• Total flexibility to cater for fluctuating workloads	• Fee scale can militate against cost efficiency in design
• Outcome is purpose-built, subject to a realistic initial brief	• Learning curve for Designers
• Industry is familiar with the option	• Loss of Client control
	• Less accountability for programme slippage
	• Potential misspecification

In-house Client, external Design and Build Contractor

This is an option favoured by smaller Authorities lacking in-house expertise or where Client needs are not specific. It can also be used to overcome the problems of severe workload peaks.

Benefits	Disbenefits
• Workload flexibility	• Outcome will not be purpose-built; that is, it will include standard elements
• Reduced lead-in time	• Life cycle costing not considered
• Possible lower capital cost	• Ease of maintenance not considered
• Optimum buildability considered as part of the design process	• Materials selection governed by cost and availability
• Cost to Client forecast accurately	• Design constrained by standard elements
	• Little Client input to design
	• No long-term involvement by Design and Build consortia
	• Very detailed brief required

In-house Client, external Design, Build, Finance and Operate Consortium

This is an option much favoured by HM Treasury, as it has no effect on the 'headline' public expenditure figures at the time of procurement.

Benefits	Disbenefits
• Can avoid capital spending controls	• Expert Client required (with expert lawyers)
• Much of the risk of failure is externalized	• Extended contract periods may make change requirements costly
• Life cycle costing fully considered by DBFO consortium	• Limited to major projects – not suitable for 'bread and butter' contracts
• Energy efficiency incentivized	• Lead-in times are invariably protracted
• Programme slippage minimized after project details finalized	• Detailed (and changing) Government criteria must be met
• Client input limited to performance specification	• Specialist appraisal teams needed to evaluate bids
	• Current capital projects obtained at the expense of future revenue costs

In-house Client, in-house Designer, external Management Contractor

This is an option that is not favoured by small Authorities with limited in-house expertise. If all parties do not pull their weight it can be stressful and expensive.

A Borough Council in the East Midlands has let two major building contracts (approx £3 million each) as JCT Management Contracts with contemporaneous in-house design of discrete work packages as a mechanism to shorten the pre-contract phase in order to meet EU Grant deadlines for Economic Development activities. This procedure utilizes in-house design and Client Agent skills while capitalizing on the Contractor's project management experience. It has been found to be a valuable way to achieve 'impossible' deadlines, but puts the staff of both partner organizations under great pressure. Programmes can be thrown off course by one key sub-contractor failing to meet promised delivery dates. Final cost outcome is also less certain than with many other forms of contract.

Benefits	Disbenefits
• Greatly reduced lead-in times (useful to meet EU deadlines) • Contractor input into buildability • Commercial incentives for good project management • Less confrontational for main parties to contract • Just-in-time design philosophy • Half-way house to full partnering	• More demanding of Design team • Less certainty of final out-turn costs • Tender delays in work packages can be critical (and expensive) • Design fees tend to be higher to reflect full-time involvement • Higher level of Client site contract management (QS/Cost Consultant)

In-house Client and Client Agent, external Framework Consultants (Designer/QS/Planning Supervisor), external Framework Contractor

This is an option which is almost Partnering. The Framework Consultants are engaged using the professional services contract at previously agreed charge-out rates which are increased from time to time on an agreed basis. Each commission has its own target fee. Similarly, each construction contract has its own tendered fixed price rates.

Framework Consultants initially tender for Framework status, and more than one Consultant may be retained. Similarly, there will be a small group of Framework Contractors who have been chosen following a submission procedure. This option lends itself to those Authorities that have a consistently high level of capital works activity.

Benefits	Disbenefits
● Client design philosophy adopted by all (for example whole life costs, ease of maintenance)	● Difficult to prove Best Value
● Trust between parties develops over time	● Needs reasonable continuity of workload to reap the benefits
● Flexibility for workload fluctuation	● Can be difficult to introduce specialisms into the team
● 'Team' shares a common learning curve	● Expert Client/Client Agent required
● Continued accountability for work	● Innovation in design and materials can be stifled
● More certainty of out-turn cost	
● Agreed sharing of risks and benefits	
● Less confrontational	

Partnering

Partnering is the next logical step. It is considered fully in Chapter 8.

Summary

As with all procurement, the choice of procurement option for single activity contracts is dependent on a number of variables: size and complexity of the project; is it a one-off?; what technical skills exist within the Authority?; and so on.

Whichever option is chosen, a good client brief is critical to success. Without it, the finished article may be a masterpiece of architecture or engineering; but if it does not fully meet the needs of the Client and end users, the procurement has failed.

In all of the options listed there is a formal contract at the heart of the procurement. The choice of which contract format to use is again dependent on the project. Whatever the choice, it is *always* preferable to use one of the tried and tested standard forms (amended if absolutely necessary) rather than a bespoke document, which is unfamiliar to both Client and Contractor.

There are, of course, variations on the options outlined. The most common variations are the *lump sum contract* and the *target cost contract*. Fixed sum contracts transfer all of the risk to the Contractor, for which the Client pays a premium in the sum charged.

A target cost contract can sit with any of the above options. In such contracts the Contractor tenders on a pre-defined basis and the accepted tender price becomes the target cost for the project. If, during the progress of the contract, savings can be achieved through value engineering/value management, these savings are shared between the Client and the Contractor on an agreed basis. Any unforeseen additional costs are similarly shared.

The sharing of both risks and benefits is taken to its logical conclusion in the option of Partnering.

8 Partnering

Partnering, as a concept, emerged as a favoured procurement option from the Egan Report 'Rethinking Construction'. Partnering is not necessarily the same as 'Partnership' in the sense of the Public/Private Partnerships, which are promoted by Government.

In a Public/Private Partnership advantage is taken of the uncontrolled availability of private finance for suitable projects; indeed, this is the key driver for such partnerships. That type of partnership may also yield benefits of better application of expertise, lower overall project cost and more realistic programming of works.

The procurement option known as Partnering is specifically aimed at obtaining these, and other, benefits, but does not depend on the availability of private finance to proceed.

What is Partnering?
There is no clearly stated formula, or set of procedures, nor any one form of contract for Partnering. Partnering is an approach. It is a culture shift away from the confrontational approach of the past. It requires a conscious decision by all of the parties to a project or service to work together for the common good.

Each partnership is unique. Partnering means working together in a way that suits the particular partners *and* which suits the particular project or service under procurement.

Although there is no standard template for Partnering, there are certain key elements which determine whether or not a particular procurement process is truly Partnering and hence likely to yield the relevant benefits.

Key words are:

- cooperation
- openness
- shared standards
- common objectives
- respect for each partner's motivation
- and, ultimately, trust.

Partnering is about sharing:

- sharing costs
- sharing risks
- sharing rewards

Most partnerships commence as a tentative experiment into Partnering on a single project and progress to a longer-term relationship of mutual trust.

Benefits of Partnering

Because Partnering draws on the strengths and expertise of the different partners in a way that is specific to the project or service, all partners can enjoy the benefits. Partnering is an ideal that should be used as the required procurement route for all complex activities and large projects. It is a process which requires all parties to the agreement to give of their best.

Specific benefits for Partnering are:

- Improved Budgeting – all partners have an input to cost projections.
- Better Programming – joint programming means more realistic programming and all partners have an interest in meeting programme dates.
- Enhanced Quality (fitness for purpose) – the close involvement of both Client and Contractor at the design stage yields dividends for the project/service end-user.
- Better Safety and Environmental Standards – genuine early involvement of the Planning Supervisor (as envisaged by the CDM Regulations) as well as the Client's Environmental adviser.
- Reduced Wasted Time – better dispute resolution.
- Reduced Contract Management Costs – better dispute resolution.
- Genuine Teamwork – optimum balance between design and buildability.
- Sharing of expertise and systems.

The Partnering process

In Project Partnering the parties to a partnering agreement would typically include the Client, Design Team (Architect, Engineer, Services Engineers, Landscape and so on), QS/Cost Consultants (Client and Contractor),

> *A small District Council Highways DLO is extending a specialist sub-contract arrangement into a long-term partnering agreement with a national roadworks contractor. The aim is to use the specialist skills and resource flexibility of the private partner together with the operational flexibility and emergency cover of the DLO to give an improved service to the public. Experience over the first year suggests that there is great potential for value-added services, but with a steep learning curve and a major culture change to be faced by the staff of both partners.*

Contractor(s), Sub-Contractor(s), Specialist Suppliers and Planning Supervisor/Safety Adviser.

The process *must* begin with commitment from the top. Top management from (at least) the Client, Contractor and Lead Designer must whole-heartedly sign up to the concept *and be seen to do so.*

From this point onwards the process is slightly fluid but must include all of the following steps if it is to succeed:

- Define the project parameters – the objectives and extent of the project are agreed between the major partners. The project is specified that it will be procured as a partnering procurement and in accordance with Partnering principles.
- Partnering workshop – a workshop is held with *all* partners in attendance. The workshop should determine the Partnering principles, what procedures are to be followed and what the role of each project partner is. The workshop will probably be foreign to the experience of many of the team members, but it is important that it is undertaken in a comprehensive manner, since all that follows will depend on the outcome of the workshop.
- Project Partnering Charter – arising out of the workshop will be a Project Partnering Charter or Vision. This will be based on the objectives of the finished project *and* on the individual objectives of the team members. Creating the Charter is an important step, because it can only be done if the objectives and motivation of each partner are known and appreciated. Once agreed, the Charter is accepted by all as a guide to both thought and actions. It should be the project's creed.
- Agreed Dispute Resolution Procedures – the key word here is 'Agreed'. Each partner should be comfortable with the procedures or at least prepared to subscribe to them. Procedures should be quick to implement and without unnecessary complexity (see Chapter 17).
- Team Approach – problem solving, risk management and innovation are all tackled on a team basis because everyone benefits.
- Team Reviews – when you are up to your neck in alligators it is difficult to remember that your initial objective was to drain the swamp. *Regular* team reviews set at the beginning of the project will enable team members to re-focus and learn from events.

Nineteen Local Authorities in the East Midlands have come together to form an Energy Partnership. Among other things, the Partnership uses its market strength, in partnership with a private sector 'Managing Agent', to achieve bulk purchasing contract discounts on the provision and installation of cavity wall insulation and other high-return energy efficiency measures for home owners in the Partnership area. Under the arrangement, which uses no public finance other than the cost of promotion activities, owner-occupiers are able to have cavity wall insulation at less than half the normal market price, with an independent quality check. Partners to the Contract are the Managing Agent and the Contractor. The public deal through the Managing Agent. Partnership Authorities act purely as facilitators.

- Final Team Review – at the end of the project, and while things are still fresh in the mind, it is important to hold a final review and 'lessons learned' session because, like Best Value, Partnering should be a process of continuing improvement.
- Teamwork still requires an appropriate and agreed management structure with defined responsibilities.

In Partnering for **service provision**, similar steps are followed. In this instance partners might include Voluntary Sector Organizations, Community Enterprises, Other Authorities (Local, Health and so on), as well as Private Sector providers.

Contract forms

There are a number of initiatives by the various contract formulation bodies aimed at providing guideline formats for Partnering. The Joint Contracts Tribunal advocates the use of its Standard Form of Contract with an accompanying statement of intent. Others identify a specific contract form as being suitable. It is said that the Engineering and Construction Contract was formulated with the Partnering concept in mind. Whatever contract form is chosen it will always be better to choose one of the industry standards, but with the Partnering Agreement being specific in the way that the Contract is to be interpreted. Having a form of contract gives a structure to the procedure and is therefore vital. Check that your partnering charter is fully compatible with the contract, as it is liable to modify the conditions in the contract (see Appendix A).

Potential problems

For an Authority to enter into a genuine partnering arrangement can present certain difficulties. True partnership involves sharing of risks and may involve Authority staff apparently undertaking work on behalf of a private sector partner. Both of these raise questions of *vires* (i.e. it is within the Authority's powers).

Standing orders, almost invariably, will have no provision for negotiated Partnering Agreements. Initial 'quasi-tender' submissions may overcome the problem in respect of the first project, but may not extend to future cooperation. A contractor procuring on behalf of the Authority should comply with the Authority's SO (see Chapter 5).

Best Value Inspectors now have the latest DETR guidance on Partnering but are likely to expect the Authority to demonstrate its value. It can be difficult to quantify the benefits of a partnering approach in a manner that meets the Best Value Auditor's requirements.

Summary

Partnering is not an easy option. For the first occasion the Authority will have to develop new processes. However, there are significant potential benefits. Trust between the parties involved in the contract will take time to develop. The process can be expedited by 'team building'.

Authorities will need to address the legal and procedural problems as well as ensuring selection of the most appropriate form of contract/partnering agreement.

Partnering is particularly beneficial where the private sector can offer skills and experience not immediately available to the Authority's own staff. Partners may also have more ready access to financial funding. If Authority procurement is to keep abreast of developments in other spheres and benefit communities, you should consider the Partnering approach. The adversarial ways of the past must give way to a more focussed and trusting approach for the future.

9 Quality

What you require from procurement of goods or services should be clearly and unambiguously specified within the appropriate contract. This allows bids to be compared in terms of their price. However, most Authorities now consider other factors rather than just the bottom line price. These other factors are covered by the overall 'quality' of the bids. In order, therefore, to ensure that tenderers include information which allows a consistent comparison, the procurement process should set out the means which will be used to assess the quality offered by the bidding organization.

External Accreditation can provide useful pointers to an organization's approach to addressing quality issues. Of the systems used, quality assurance through the ISO 9000 series is probably the most common. A criticism of this form of quality assurance is that whilst it addresses consistency of approach it does not in itself guarantee quality. Similarly, Investors In People focuses on the way an organization behaves towards its workforce, often its greatest asset. Some external accreditation systems effectively combine the two approaches.

Health and Safety are always important considerations in procurement and ones which the procurer cannot take for granted. Bidders should be required to set out their approach to health and safety clearly in their bids, including the company's health and safety policy. If the work involves construction, then specific method statements on the Construction, Design and Management Regulations (CDM) may be requested. Other particular types of work may well have their own specific health and safety legislation. You should ensure that you understand exactly what health and safety measures are required, and that they will be met.

The level of *Resources* available to bidders is important because it can indicate their ability to cope with the contract, especially if, for whatever reason, it does not go as planned. The financial standing of tenderers should always be checked using one or more of the various methods available to Authorities. The size of the organization may be a good indicator of its ability to provide any necessary backup when things go wrong. Does the company have the correct skills mix to cover all the work? Will some of it have to be sub-contracted out to others? You should seek to appoint an organization on the basis of its positive approach to quality issues and the way in which it instils this in any sub-contractors. Size is also relevant in respect of the proportion of annual turnover represented by the particular procurement exercise; too big a proportion puts both contractor and contract at risk.

Any organization's *Ability* to deliver the desired outcomes will depend on a number of critical areas. These desired outcomes might include not only the finished product, but also:

- the process that will be used to achieve it
- completing the service within budget
- finishing on time.

The procurement process should ascertain how the project would be managed. What are the lines of communication within the company? Is there a clear definition of who will be responsible for what? The proposal could include a 'project plan', which confirms the tenderers awareness of the project's demands and his ability to manage it successfully.

Another matter which might need clarification is the form of budgetary control that the contractor will exercise, particularly if the contract requires direct control over an Authority budget. It may also be useful to establish the manner in which the bidding company anticipates developing a beneficial relationship with the Authority.

External references will undoubtedly be useful in confirming the tenderer's answers to many of the issues above, particularly in assessing a company's financial standing. 'Technical' references obtained from current or recent clients will help in assessing ability. But past performance is of course no guarantee as to future performance, and references should be treated only as a guide.

Many Authorities now require contracts to take a far more sustainable approach to *Environmental* and *Ecological issues*. A contractor's approach to this important subject might be considered under the broad heading of bid quality. At pre-qualification stage, prospective tenderers could be asked to confirm their previous experience of undertaking contracts whilst respecting these issues. Their bids could also include environmental statements setting out their general approach and specifically their approach to recycling and conservation, for example.

Customer care has always been important to any successful organization. Many Authorities have widened the definition of *customer* to include third parties affected by any of the activities involved in executing the contract. Whilst contracts should specify what is expected from a successful contractor, it is also reasonable to expect contractors to state how they will deal with customer care specific to their own proposed way of working. This would normally include demonstrating their previous experience in keeping the public informed and may involve the need for both consultation and presentation skills.

Finally, previous experience of working for an Authority will help any organization understand the need for sensitivity, particularly when carrying out work that may be disruptive to the public. Contractors may be asked to explain how they would undertake the required activities with due consideration to those affected by them.

10 Value for money

General

Obtaining value involves more than accepting the lowest price bid. We describe two financially based techniques, but then expand from this approach to a more comprehensive value for money strategy.

Benefit–cost analysis

Frequently, decisions on whether to proceed with a particular project are taken on the basis of the ratio between financial benefits and costs. At its simplest this may be assessed in terms of the payback period required to recover the project costs. Such a technique has the advantages of being relatively quick, easy to understand and adaptable when, for example, deciding the priority order of several schemes.

A more thorough benefit–cost analysis would involve an assessment of capital and revenue costs over the estimated life of a project.

> *Examples of life expectancies are:*
>
> - *Heat distribution mains: 40 years*
> - *Highways construction: 40 years*
> - *Pre-formed building cladding systems: 20–30 years*
> - *Traditional brickwork: 100 years*
> - *Coast protection: 20 years*
> - *Buildings: 60 years*
> - *Housing and dwellings: 80 years*

> *HM Treasury's Guidance:*
>
> *The Discount Rate is **not** the inflation rate but is the investment 'premium' over and above inflation. Provided inflation for all costs is approximately equal, it is normal practice to exclude inflation effects when undertaking LCC analysis.*
>
> *Guidance No. 35* Life Cycle Costing, *published by HM Treasury (issued April 1992 but likely to be shortly superseded).*

Future costs are discounted to provide a net present value (NPV) before the benefits and costs are compared. It is important not to confuse discounting and inflation.

A benefit to cost ratio of 1.0 or more indicates a financially worthwhile scheme. The priority order of several schemes can be decided in terms of the highest benefit to cost ratio. The financial benefits of some projects (for example coast protection) are hard to assess. For many others there is perhaps no financial benefit, but rather a social or environmental benefit to which it is difficult to give financial values. Techniques for implying value (for example the value of time saved) have been developed, but should be used with care.

Whole life costing

Project evaluation is incomplete unless whole life costing is taken into account. The appraisal technique known as whole life costing is not new, but is rarely used for other than major contracts. One reason for this is perhaps that the cost of the appraisal itself can become disproportionally high in relation to the actual contract costs themselves.

> *Whole-life cost takes into account all aspects of cost over time, including for example capital, maintenance, management, operating and disposal costs.*
>
> *Financial Information Service, Volume 7 – Procurement, published by CIPFA.*

The costing exercise should include all costs and incomes accruing over the life of the project. The costs of initiating the project should be included, such as land acquisition, the costs of the procurement exercise itself, head office costs (including overheads) and any project supervision costs during either provision or use. The appraisal techniques should attempt to quantify the effects of continuous improvement measured in financial terms.[1]

Whole life costing requires estimates of both capital and on-going budgets. It therefore demands coordination between the initiators of a project with those who will manage it in the future. The apparent advantage of simply accepting the lowest tender price for a specified product ignores the differences in durability and operation. This tends to discourage the assessment of different designs, different procurement routes or different quality products. For example, a higher quality product or a more expensive initial outlay could produce lower maintenance costs, a longer life or a higher residual value with overall savings. Similarly, a different procurement route may result in savings on procurement, design or administration charges that could allow a greater asset value to be provided. The Audit Commission[2] found that these transaction costs were significant with CCT contracts. Indeed, client transaction costs for CCT contracts were as much as 10% of the annual value of contracts.

We would strongly recommend whole life costing (even if simplified) as part of the assessment process.

HM Treasury, within its series of publications on Procurement Guidance, states:

Best Value for Money is the optimum combination of whole life cost and quality to meet the customer's requirements.

Procurement Guidance No 2: Value for Money in Construction Procurement, published by HM Treasury quoting 'Setting New Standards – A Strategy for Government Procurement', Cm 2480.

Procurement should aim to achieve overall Value for Money, not just the lowest initial tender price.

Value management reviews

Value for Money seeks to achieve the most desirable balance of three elements:

- whole life cost
- quality
- customer's requirements.

---

1 BS ISO 15686: *Buildings and Constructed Assets - Service Life Planning - Part 1: General Principles*
2 To buy or not to buy, I&DeA published by LGA 1999 p. 21 quoting 'Realising the benefits of competition', Audit Commission 1993

Each of these elements should be assessed. Procurement seeks to optimize each of these. The achievement of Value for Money demands quite complex decisions. Indeed, there are numerous factors that must be considered in the decision-making process.

The key decisions can be facilitated by standard procedures, flowcharts (Figure 10.1), standing orders, checklists, procurement models and so on.

The decision to be made in procurement can be complex and interact with each other. To ensure that decisions will achieve the Best Value, periodic management reviews should be undertaken. The reviews are more likely to realize real improvements if someone, not otherwise involved, leads the review and the whole partnership team contribute. 'Value Engineering' is a particular form of review that seeks to identify better materials or methods of delivering the specified service. Whilst Value Engineering is consistent with the aims of Best Value, procurement reviews should extend to all aspects of the process. Thus reviews should be a feature of the procurement process, should be programmed at key stages, or fixed intervals, and should be recorded. The output from these reviews should be translated into improvements to the way procurement is conducted in future.

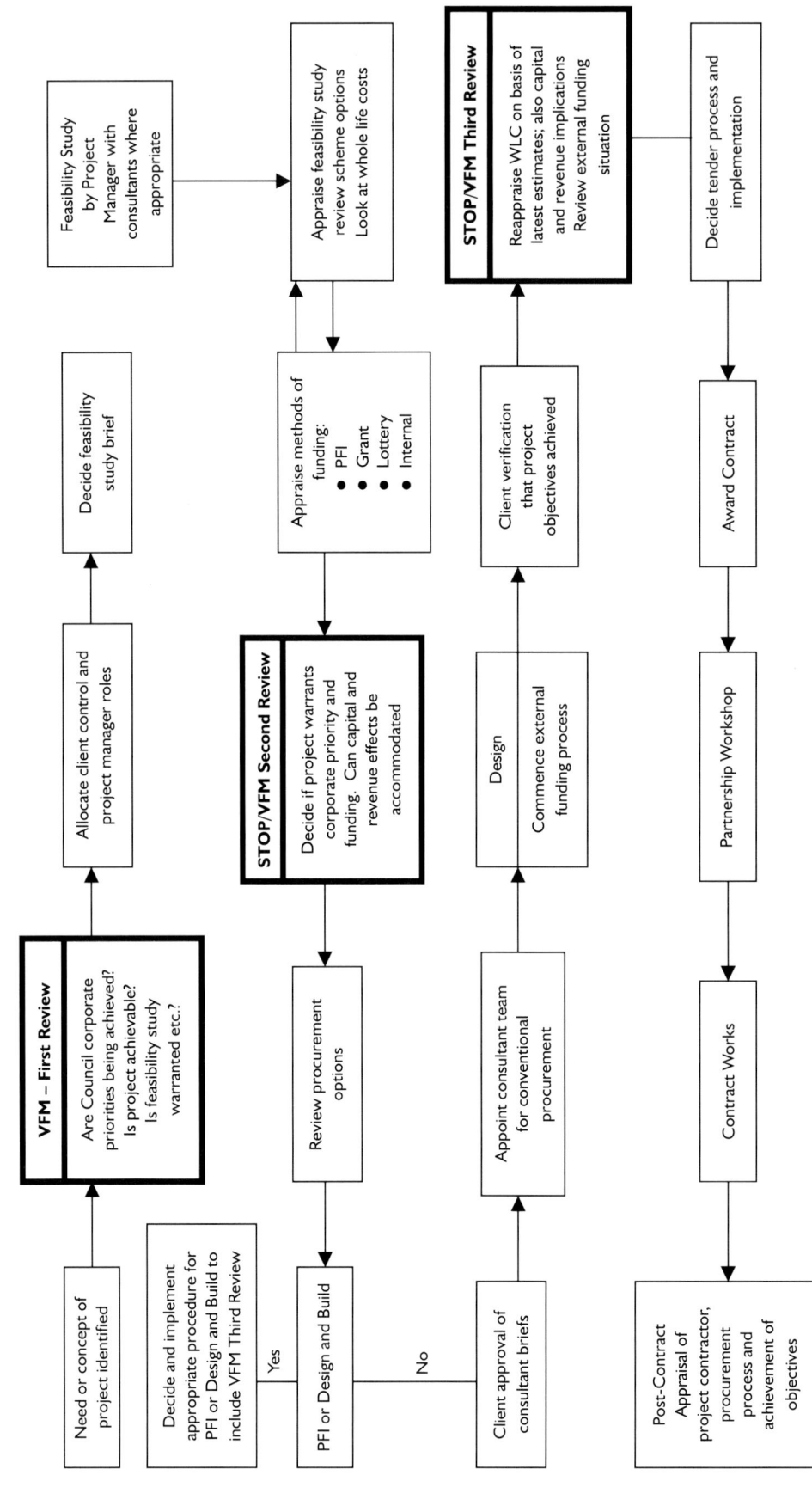

Figure 10.1 Example of a VFM framework for major projects.

11 Length of contract

What is the most appropriate length of your contract? Clearly you need to match the length of contract with the time-scale necessary to achieve the required outcome together with the level of investment and training necessary.

There is not an ideal formula for determining the length of a contract. It is very much a question of determining the most appropriate 'horse for the particular course'. Contract periods vary with the type of work and services provided. For Term Contracts where the contractor has to provide significant 'up front' investment a contract period of 10–15 years is not unusual. Indeed, where very significant investment is required, periods of up to 25 years are adopted. A maintenance or minor contract, where investment is limited to enabling the contractor to fulfil this contract, is likely to be no more than three or four years in length.

For single-purpose contracts, such as designing or building a new facility, the duration of the contract should match the reasonable rate of progress to completion. A shorter contract length will result in higher costs, justifiable only if the Authority has an immutable need for an early completion. Good practice would do one of the following:

- Ask Contractors' advice (in other words consult them) before formal tenders are issued.
- Ask tenderers to specify the time they require to perform the service as part of their bid. The Authority should indicate the 'weight' they intend to give to this factor in the evaluation of the tenders.

Whatever the service, there is highly likely to be interaction and possibly interdependence on other services. Service contracts do not stand in isolation. Each should be seen as part of the Authority's overall service delivery. It follows that contracts should fit within a strategy. Some would argue that contracts should be co-terminus, so as to provide stability and consistent relationships between concurrent contractors (such as refuse collection and vehicle maintenance). Others prefer periodic renewal of contracts, so as to avoid sudden peaks in procurement activity. Some prefer several discrete contracts to enable a variety of contractors to tender. Others argue for single, comprehensive service contracts. There are benefits and disadvantages in each case, but the Authority's strategy should be the result of thoughtful and careful consideration. Occasional strategy reviews will ensure the continued robustness of the strategy.

At the time of preparing the contract, the procurement manager should analyse the scope of the contract and the anticipated output and outcomes resulting from the contract. From this he or she should decide the probable level of investment and the time-scale necessary to achieve the required results.

Set out below are some examples of contract length, types of contract, and issues to be considered when determining the length of contract term.

Contracts for professional services
Individual commissions
- Time specified for completion of individual commissions.
- No new office setup. Delivered from existing offices.
- Little or no staff recruitment necessary. Commission delivered from within existing resources.
- No new training necessary.
- Little or no new capital investment necessary by contractor.

Term Contracts
- Five to seven years.
- Possible relocation of office accommodation.
- Installation and provision of new IT links from contractor to client.
- Capital investment by contractor necessary to fulfil contract.
- Some staff recruitment likely.
- Mobilization period necessary prior to start of contract.
- Length of contract allows client opportunity to review scope of arrangements and aspects of service delivery to meet changes in demand on a regular basis.
- Length of contract allows contractor to develop team over a series of projects to partner (formally or informally) with client.

Contracts for works
Site specific contracts
- Actual length of contract determined by size and complexity of scheme.
- Allows full advantage to be taken of market forces at time of tendering.
- Lump sum or target cost contracts.
- Little or no capital investment necessary by Contractor to complete contract other than that associated with the normal running of the Contractor's business.
- Minimal staff recruitment and training necessary.
- Minimal mobilization period.

Three to five year contracts (for example Term Maintenance or Minor Works Contracts)

- Little or no up-front financial investment necessary.
- Generally a 'schedule of rates' type of contract with prices updated for inflation and so on.
- Payments based on measured work.
- Short length of contract allows client opportunity to regularly review service and to meet changing demands and conditions.
- Some relocation of office or depot accommodation may be necessary and this will be reflected in the contract rates.

Five to fifteen year contracts (for example Partnered contracts)

- Significant 'up front' financial investment by Contractor probable.
- Term must be long enough for Contractor to make this investment viable.
- Appropriate mobilization period must be allowed – this could be several months.
- Office relocation and depot relocation probably necessary.
- Installation and provision of new IT links from Contractor to Client.
- Some staff recruitment and training likely.
- Contract must be flexible enough to meet changing conditions and developments during the contract period, and demands not foreseen when contract signed.
- Partnered Contractor available to be involved with the development and implementation of innovative solutions.
- Long-term contract may restrict Client in reviewing service delivery and meeting changes in demands on that service.
- Contract likely to be based on quality as well as price.
- Payment based on quality of performance as well as quantity.
- Key Performance Indicators necessary to monitor performance.
- Possible difficulties in terminating contract prior to end of term.
- Market research necessary during tendering period to ensure potential partners are able to deliver investment and benefits required from long-term contract.
- Contract preparation time can be lengthy.
- Once contract let, time is needed to develop partnering culture.
- Partnered Contractor available to be involved with projects at design stage.

Over fifteen year contracts (for example DBFO or PFI contracts)

- Contract term will be determined by length of time necessary to recoup financial investment.
- Contractor involved at design stage.
- Some office and depot relocation may be necessary.
- Known operating costs.
- Lengthy contract preparation time.
- Difficulties in terminating contract arrangements.
- Up-front finance required by contractor.

In summary, therefore, short-term contracts can provide cost-effective solutions, where the contractor is not required to make major capital investment in premises, plant or equipment, whilst longer term contracts provide the contractor with continuity of work and the opportunity for long-term planning and investment. They also provide a climate for the contractor to develop local investment and joint initiatives for innovation, providing an opportunity of involvement with the local community and for the contractor to establish a local identity.

12 Evaluation of tenders

Process

The evaluation techniques used to choose a successful tenderer depend on a number of factors, such as services covered, political sensitivity, value, standing orders and conditions of contract. Consider each tender individually and determine the most appropriate level of evaluation for that tender.

Comparative assessment is easier if a Standard Schedule of Rates such as the National Schedule (NSR) is used as a benchmark. A simple quotation for low-value work could involve a quick written confirmation of a price agreed over the telephone. A complex tender for work worth many millions will involve a much more rigorous approach. Every evaluation must be seen to be open, honest and fair. Records of decisions taken and clear documentation should be available for an audit trail.

Whatever route is chosen, it is best discussed during the development of the tender documents. The simple quotation will be governed by rules set down in Standing Orders and where applicable, the EC Procurement Rules (see Chapter 4). For all formal tenders, however, the documents themselves have to describe the evaluation method. 'The employer does not bind himself to accept the lowest, or any, tender.' With the need to prove best value it is important to describe the evaluation technique fully. Is 'quality' going to be scored? What criteria will the 'quality' aspects be judged against? Are there any specific areas of priority such as treatment of people who might transfer to the successful tenderer under the Transfer of Undertakings and Protection of Employment regulations (TUPE)?

Probity

Probity is defined in the *Oxford English Dictionary* as 'uprightness, honesty, integrity'. In the public sector it is the foundation of the financial and decision-making process. It is not enough to say that a procedure is 'proper': it must be seen to be from start to finish.

Authorities must ensure that all staff involved in procurement maintain the highest standards of integrity. The Authority's SO should be explained to them along with the implications of not working within the rules. Requiring two signatures on every invoice is a simple but coarse way of protecting individuals from accusations of impropriety. Instilling probity into employees from the start of their involvement in purchasing work will protect them and the organization.

SO define rules about the varying procurement procedures needed for certain values of work. Aligned with that is the need to inform individuals of their personal delegations. This means that expenditure is dealt with at the most appropriate level and protects employees and the organization.

Elected councillors are the custodians of public funds, and it is they who are responsible for its proper use. They therefore approve the procedures and rules used by officers for procurement. Often this is enough to reassure them that the public money is being spent appropriately, but with more sensitive expenditure they need greater involvement.

It is important to remember that Authorities can only function through delegating the power to carry out the majority of functions to their officers. Historically, individual councillors did not have personal delegated authority; only committees could make decisions as a group. Committees then delegated the detail to the chief officer who subsequently delegated the responsibility downward throughout the organization as appropriate.

This has changed with the introduction of Cabinet government, and now individual councillors have the decision-making powers of committees. Chief Officers and the cabinet members have to work closely together and Standing Orders are changing to reflect the new roles.

Receipt, analysis and evaluation

The procurement process operates through the Standing Orders, individual delegations and agreed office procedures. From these, officers know how to procure works and services in an open and honest manner. Assessing the provider of a service from the quotations or tenders received can be complex and there are a variety of methods available to do this.

There is a wide range of techniques available for evaluation of submissions, but not all are appropriate for each assessment. It is very important to consider the extent of the assessment process as early as possible in the procurement time-scale so as not to waste time unduly on over-intricate or inappropriate systems.

Receipt is the point at which probity must be seen to be upheld and so independently controlled (see Chapter 5). Robust systems must be set up to prevent accusations of tampering. Quotations and tenders may be submitted by post, personal delivery or courier. They will come in spread over a period of time, so consideration must be given to secure storage. Often the tender documents will include a self-addressed envelope for their return because the tenderer should not be identifiable from the outside of the envelope. It is very important that for all bids for work, except small quotations, they should be returned to and kept securely by an independent person.

Confidentiality

All information supplied is commercially confidential and must not be passed between competing organizations. The fewer people who know the details within quotations and tenders, the lower the risk of confidentiality being breached.

For small quotations that confirm discussions held over the telephone, it is often sufficient for these to be addressed to the manager of the team responsible for the work. For larger quotations and tenders, at least two people should be present at tender opening. One should be the independent person responsible for the safe keeping of the returned tender envelopes; the other could be a person of adequate responsibility who is involved with the assessment. Often an elected councillor is also present, such as the Chairperson of the relevant committee.

A Tender Return Form should be completed at opening time. As each envelope is opened the appropriate tender sum is written against the company name on the form and the people present sign the tender against the place where the tender sum has been taken. Those tenderers who did not return their bid should be indicated on the form as well.

Late tenders need to be treated carefully and the date and time of receipt written on both the envelope and the tender document. Consideration needs to be given as to whether the tender is opened or not, and Standing Orders should clarify this (see Chapter 5).

Assessment

There are three phases to an initial assessment:

- An arithmetical check to ensure that the tender sum as submitted is correct and that the bids conform to the requirements of the Instructions to tenderers.
- An examination of prices and rates.
- An evaluation or comparison of rates and prices between tenders to determine whether any errors or misunderstandings have occurred between the various organizations.

SO will lay down the organization's rules for the treatment of non-conforming tenders, errors in arithmetic, omissions or misunderstandings. Generally such bids can be discarded, held to price or amended by the tenderer, depending on the circumstances.

For simple one-off, short-term contracts it is often enough to have carried out an initial assessment and determined the lowest priced conforming tender. For more complex contracts which cover services or will operate for a number of years, other elements must be brought into the assessment to decide which tenderer is going to provide the best value to the organization over the whole term.

Risk assessment of the rates and prices should be undertaken so as to understand the strategy used in pricing the document. Each organization will use a different process to prepare its prices and rates. It is very important to use the tendered prices in a variety of scenarios, which reflect possible occurrences throughout the life of the contract. As an example, in a contract covering winter maintenance, try pricing a variety of winter scenarios from no snow and ice to, say, a three-week snow emergency.

Although the bills of quantities will have been prepared as accurately as possible, are there any items that might increase or decrease significantly? You should estimate how that affects the outcome. Consider the effect of one-off payments within the contract. You should not forget to take into account the loss of interest to the Authority as a whole if you guarantee a particular level of cash flow to a contractor. It may benefit your budget, but actually lose the Authority more money overall.

You should also take into account the impact of annual price increases that are built into the contract. How have these changed when compared with inflation? What impact will these have on the overall cost?

Net present value

In all cases where the contract includes price fluctuation clauses, it is essential that you compare the tendered prices on a standard basis. Discounting the costs to a common base year will enable you to make a real comparison and will take into account the impact of alternative scenarios. The figure in the bids should be checked with the whole life costing model (see Chapter 10).

Quality/service delivery

During the preparation of the tender documents you will have decided what level of assessment you need to choose the successful contractor. If you have decided to include an element of 'quality' or 'service delivery' in the assessment there will be a section in the tender document describing what is expected of each tenderer for their submission.

An evaluation sheet might support the questions asked in the Evaluation of Tender Mechanisms (see the exhibit at the end of this chapter). Before tenders are sought, the various criteria are percentage weighted by a group of senior managers who are in a position to decide the relative importance that each criterion should have. The total of the criteria weights should be 100. This involves choosing the emphasis to be put on, say, Service Delivery and Competence, compared with Transitional Arrangements.

Each tenderer should supply the documents requested with responses to the relevant questions. These responses need to be assessed by a group of people who are independent of the checks on the financial aspects of the bids. Each person independently assesses each quality submission and gives the various criteria a score between 0 and 5 (0 being 'did not provide an answer', 5 being 'all aspects covered and 100% satisfactory'). The various scores are then averaged across all the assessors and the criteria weights applied to the averages. From the resulting table comes a total weighted score for each tenderer, and this should provide a subjective indication of the variations in quality of the submissions.

Some Authorities ask tenderers to prepare method statements to show how they would undertake the contract. Method statements are required under safety legislation, but these do not need to be prepared in advance of the appointment of the successful Contractor. Indeed, no form of method statement should be sought from tenderers unless the system of working is an essential element in choosing the Contractor. Rarely do such situations arise, but if proposed methods are to be part of the quality submission, tenderers should be made aware of both the information required and how it will be judged in the assessment process.

So you have two pieces of information available to pick the best value contractor: 'Financial' and 'Quality'. Final judgement of the best bid could be made on the basis of these two pieces of information using professional experience. There are two further ways of using this information to help with the assessment: the Price Discounting Model and the Prior Overall Weighting Model. These allow the Price/Quality ratio to be varied to see whether increasing quality changes the ranking of the various tenders.

Before a final decision is made, there may have been questions arising from the analysis which need response from the tenderers. Extreme care should be exercised to make certain that any points of clarification that are raised with one tenderer do not put them at an advantage or indeed a disadvantage. During the tender period, great care will have been taken to ensure that all tenderers have the same information, and it is important to maintain that concept during the tender evaluation.

All evaluation models are simple tools to help those responsible for selecting contractors to make a Best Value judgement that can be defended when challenged. It is quite likely that one or two losing tenderers will want to discuss the tender process and where they fell short. Managers must be prepared to answer challenging questions, but as long as the process has been robust and the decision seen to be fair then there is no need for concern.

Award

The selection of contractors is often a responsibility delegated to a Chief Officer, but in certain situations it may be prudent, or indeed necessary, to report the process to a committee and enable them to make a formal decision. In this case confidentiality needs to be maintained with the various tenderers referred to as Tenderer A, B, C and so on, especially as these reports are available to the general public before the committee convenes.

The committee may also need to consider the budgetary implications of a tender, as the final result is likely to be at variance from the available budget. A decision will then have to be made as to whether to proceed with a contract or not to award at all.

Once all elements have been considered and an award is made, it is important to inform all tenderers of the result. Normal protocol allows for the successful Contractor and the Contractor's tender sum to be announced along with the names of the other tenderers in alphabetical order and the tendered sums in numerical order.

Partnering

The process of selecting a 'partner' for a partnering contract (see Chapter 8) will take a very similar pattern. The characteristics which the Authority believes would achieve a successful partnership should be annotated and included in the assessment matrix. Again, potential partners need to know what is expected of them so that they can make a relevant submission as part of their bid.

Evaluation of Tender Mechanism

Contract for Engineering and Transportation Services			Members of Tender Board					
Quality weighting								
Cost weighting								
Quality								
Quality criteria	Criteria data – references refer to Instructions for Tendering 6.1	Criteria weight %	Organization A		Organization B		Organization C	
			Score	Weighted score	Score	Weighted score	Score	Weighted score
(i) Innovation	c, d, e, g, i, k, l							
(ii) Partnering	c							
(iii) Service Delivery and Competence	d, e, g, i, j, k, l							
(iv) Terms and Conditions including Pensions	f							
(v) Consultant's organization and experience	d, e, i, j, l							
(vi) Transitional Arrangements	e, l							
(vii) Quality and Quality Management Systems	d, i							
(viii) Added staff CVs for management or other specialist services in a senior capacity	d							
(ix) Proposals to deal with customer care, VFM, Value Engineering and Best Value	d, i, j, l							
(x) Future Strategy and Stability	g, h, l							
TOTALS								
Cost Scores								
Financial model evaluation								
Value of assets								
Notes								

(1) Other information outlined in the tender, such as alternative tenders, may be used as criteria data.

13 E-procurement

The future

The UK Government has set a national target for 90% of its correspondence to be electronic by 2008. Many successful organizations are making extensive use of electronic communication over the Internet and by email. Many are convinced that this is the future for 'shopping' for their services and thereby generating work for themselves.

Local Authorities have in the main been slow to pick up on the benefits that e-business can bring. Their caution may be because of the financial commitment needed before benefits are seen. For commercial organizations, the benefits are greater potential turnover and profit. For the public sector it is improved communication and service, which should be more attuned to the customers' needs. Proving that the investment has produced the promised benefits is therefore harder for the public sector, which is better at measuring inputs to a service, such as applied budgets, rather than outputs, such as improvements to quality of life.

Nevertheless, the Government's targets extend to local authorities as well as their own departments, and hence Authorities must take action to meet the challenge. The regime of Best Value provides the framework to tackle this issue and the catalyst for a step change in procurement using e-business.

Problems

Protectionists within organizations argue that allowing greater access to systems opens up the potential for infiltration and deliberate vandalism of sensitive information. Such systems should never be put in jeopardy. In the e-world, commercial business has shown that such problems exist, but can be overcome. The risks of unauthorized access must be assessed and dealt with by proper management systems. Authority staff should be encouraged to take a progressive attitude to expanding availability of services.

So far the numbers of people trusting enough to pay their bills over the Internet or visiting information sites is comparatively small. Some would argue that investment in the computer systems is not worthwhile. However, the growth in businesses and families with connection to the Internet is rising rapidly. With the demise of analogue television, every household will have digital, and hence Internet, capability. As more online shopping facilities become available, 'ordinary people' will see the benefits. The demand for doing business by electronic means is likely to soar.

Many Authorities are working together with commercial organizations to develop electronic communication and e-commerce. At least one large County Council has already placed its supplies ordering service on its Intranet site and its staff can place their orders online. Another has developed a Works Ordering system with its term contractor so that every client office can send orders direct across the wide area network and receive completed, measured invoices back for payment. Sufficient security has been provided to enable the term contractor, agents and the client authority to have a live system that can be trusted. The New Roads and Street Works Act 'opening notices' sent by utility companies to the relevant Highway Authority went electronic in 2000. Now the manual systems are a rarity. Similarly electronic street lighting maintenance systems exist across the country, handling information about the inventory without recourse to paper exchanges.

In many cases all that is lacking is the confidence to let the public in. Could the public post their street lighting complaints on the Internet so that the report automatically gets logged in the system?

Could the public access a Web site which tells them the name of the organization responsible for remedying their particular problem and provides the means of communicating that complaint directly to the people who effect the remedy?

Contract documents have historically been issued on paper, and our procurement systems perpetuate this. Yet most documents are now produced by word processor, bills of quantities by spreadsheet and drawings by CAD (computer-aided design), so the act of transferring the documents back to paper is a retrograde step. It is logical to put them on a CD-ROM or on a Web site for the tenderers to download. The final difficulty is authentication, but it is quite feasible to use digital signatures instead of written ones. A read-only CD means that the core document is protected, giving necessary reassurance that it has not been tampered with.

The change to e-business demands leadership and radical thought to overcome the very valid concerns of those responsible for probity. Without leadership and drive, ideas could be stifled and opportunities lost. Authorities can make a major leap into the future by embracing the facility of electronic communications with the public and commercial organizations to meet the growing expectation for improvements in services. The public is rapidly developing its ability to use the technology now available. Their expectations of access to information as individuals or during their business lives will demand changes of Authorities. Those Authorities who fall behind in e-information will soon find their satisfaction ratings dropping when compared with their neighbours. Government undoubtedly will reward those Authorities who have the highest public satisfaction ratings.

Business will expect contracts and orders to be issued electronically, backed up with automated invoicing and payment, thereby improving cash flow. Authorities, for their part, must develop effective systems and treat e-business as the normal way of trading and communication.

Authorities should seek to make the most of the e-business opportunities. But the change to e-business is both an expensive investment and involves reengineering the business processes. There is much to gain, but much can go wrong. The wise Authority will consult widely, both internally and externally, on the services available and on future processes so as to ensure they minimize waste and maximize effectiveness of investment. Sharing ideas is an essential part of achieving Government targets. There is little to be gained by steadfastly treading the path you have always gone down when someone else already knows a better, quicker or safer way.

Targets

The Government's targets are clear. Authorities should develop practical achievable targets of their own. Development should not be led by the 'computer people', but by the Authority's established leadership. All procurement staff should be involved in defining and developing the improvements. Otherwise, paper systems will continue to be used as the trusted back-up.

14 Thinking ahead – longer term consequences

Introduction

If the purpose of a sound procurement strategy is to achieve the right service at the right price, then a part of this process will involve an assessment of the whole lifespan of the service contract. But that is not the end of the matter. Not only will the Authority be concerned to ensure the efficient and effective operation of the service acquired, but it will have an ongoing commitment even when the initial contract comes to an end. In practice, we find few managers look beyond the immediate contract arrangements. However, what is done now may well prejudice the future. It is important to think ahead, and so we set out some of the key issues.

> *The manager should think first and act second. The manager who does not think is **a danger**, both to himself and his organization.*
>
> *Ben Hier*, The Manager as a Decision Thinker.

'Purpose-span'

Capital projects are traditionally costed over a design life based on the structural integrity of the components. However, the increasing pace of technological change, new working practices and changing social and political attitudes means that the purpose of a product/service should be appraised and an assessment made as to when that purpose (or use) is likely to be significantly altered. This may suggest a different lifespan from that traditionally selected.

Contract rationalization

Your Authority is likely to let several contracts, so the benefits likely to accrue in terms of direct contract costs, procurement costs or contract administration costs from either the combination or perhaps the subdivision of contracts should be analysed. Clearly you will decide the length of individual Term Contracts. This involves long-term planning. As an example, an Authority decided to reduce four Term Contracts for grounds maintenance into two or three. This could not be achieved easily, since the original contracts ended in different years. No previous thought had been given to such possible rationalization.

Contractor availability

In many segments of supply, Authorities may be the largest purchaser of materials, expertise or skills in their area. Procurement strategies may heavily influence whether some local contractors or suppliers will continue to exist. This not only needs to be taken into account in terms of future competition and hence the likely levels of tender prices, but can also have significant economic effects on the Authority area. Size of contracts can either help to maintain smaller companies or could assist the larger national companies to move towards a monopoly position. Economists tell us that the competitor's aim is monopoly. Monopolies (or cartels) can choose the prices they charge clients. As any sector of industry or commerce moves toward monopolies and agglomerations, Authority contracts become far more expensive. The greater the specialization involved in the contract, the greater risk of dependency on a single supplier.

Selection of procurement method

The Best Value process will accelerate the recent trends to review the actual procurement methods that your Authority uses. Such review needs to be completed long before any new tendering process is begun. Before letting any contract, Authorities should also have considered how their preferred procurement system would impinge on the ability of the Authority to:

- assess different procurement options in the future
- pursue joint ventures
- develop partnering opportunities.

The review may indicate a need to maintain a minimum level of work for in-house resources if such resources are regarded as strategically critical.

Sustainability

Very few major contracts will now proceed without a comprehensive environmental impact assessment. However, the assessment often concentrates simply on the period of the contract. A complete procurement strategy will introduce to the process an evaluation of the contract in terms of both the short- and long-term environmental effects. You should review potential fuel and materials usage in terms of the more environmentally friendly technologies now available and also consider such matters as transportation costs stimulated both by and as a result of the contract. For example, the increasing fashion for 'quality' materials in buildings and town centre streets involves the quarrying of natural materials, both in this country and overseas. Can we justify the environmental damage in one location to enhance the environment in another?

We need to reflect on the situation when the project life is over, particularly if this is a major construction project. How best can the environment be protected? Can an environmentally friendly project be achieved by recycling or restoration?

Rising costs

Your Authority is able to afford a long-term contract now. But what about the future? You should check the consequences of the price rise indices built into the contract. Finance available to Authorities has diminished over the last several years, but the demand for service has risen. What are the consequences of your Authority being less able or willing to finance your particular Term Contract in the future?

PFI costs

The use of private, rather than public, finance seems an attractive option. Indeed, Government is advocating the use of private finance through partnering arrangements. Nothing is free. Private finance costs more than public money. Whilst not obvious in the short-run, extra cost will become evident unless offset by commensurate savings through efficiency. Maybe those savings could be achieved without recourse to private sector finance.

Democratic control

Local Government in the UK is still a democratic institution. Elected members make choices for Authorities, albeit under increasing Government restrictions. Consider two scenarios:

- The political control of your Authority changes. Would your contract meet the new political objectives? What are the consequences? Is the contract period chosen to frustrate legitimate political changes?
- If an increasing proportion of services are subject to long-term partnering arrangements, what opportunities remain for democratic choice?

Staffing

Authorities benefit from impartial advice. Advice from any sector, even from partnering contractors, will have an element of bias. Without experienced staff, the bias in advice received may go unnoticed. Authorities must continue to have access to independent and impartial advice. Quality staff are the surest way of securing quality advice. To transfer all experienced staff to a contractor will lead to problems for the Authority.

Services are organized on a critical mass basis. The reallocation of key staff to the private sector will result in a loss of knowledge within the Authority and subsequent disintegration of professional teams. Whilst the effects may not be apparent in the short term, the loss of ability to develop new services so as to respond to the changing environment may well become self-evident in due time.

Procurement decisions should be influenced by:

- *The views of users and members on how services should develop*
- *The benefits of partnering in service development*
- *The avoidance of confrontational contracting in favour of relational arrangements*
- *The better management of risk*
- *The potential for innovation in the provision of services*
- *The opportunities to improve management skills*
- *The ability to protect the interests of staff.*

Bill Ogley, Chief Executive at New Local Government Network Conference 1999, as quoted in Approaches to Best Value Services: to buy or not to buy?, I&DeA, *published by the Local Government Association.*

Summary

All the points made in this chapter may be simply summarized as emphasizing the need to think beyond the immediate contract letting. Utilizing the whole life costing approach (see Chapter 10) will often concentrate on factors within the lifespan of the contract or the product being provided. Wider vision, sometimes of a socio-economic nature, is frequently required. There is little benefit to be gained from cheap contracts if, at the end of the contract, the Authority is left with a building (such as a leisure centre or council housing stock), plant (of any type) or vehicles (such as gritting lorries or refuse lorries) that it cannot afford to renew or replace. Short-term savings can become long-term problems and may actually lead to subsequent contracts being very unattractive to tenderers or hugely expensive for Authorities to continue. Even in the short term, such contracts could restrict flexibility or the ability of the Authority to be innovative.

15 Other issues

Procurement, especially of complex services, is likely to raise several apparently peripheral issues. However, failure to recognize and resolve these issues can result in delays and increased costs to the Authority. We list and comment on some of the issues which have become contentious in particular cases.

Training

Authorities used to be a prime source of 'on the job' training. The increase in the outsourcing of services could well reduce training opportunities. Term Contracts, in particular, could include the requirement to provide relevant training opportunities so as to ensure those employed on the contract have the necessary expertise to deliver the services effectively and efficiently. However, the contract should not require unreasonable levels of training, unrelated to the contract itself.

Similarly, the selection of suitable contractors may include the availability of skilled and experienced people to carry out the works. However, an overly prescriptive definition of training scheme requirements maybe construed as uncompetitive. Under Section 19 of the Local Government Act 1999 and subsequent guidance,[1] training may need to be considered in evaluating tenders and letting contracts.

Flexibility

Many Authorities tend to prefer 'input' specifications in their contracts, whereby the standards of 'workmanship' and materials are clearly set out. Such an approach assures:

- contractors are competing on an equal basis
- the Authority can be certain of receiving the specified service.

1 DETR circular 02/2001

> *One District Council is addressing the lack of public finance for improvement of the housing stock by supporting, through advice and officer time, a free-standing, community-based, charitable company. The company proposes to install, maintain, and operate a community heating network using combined heat and power to give affordable warmth to every resident in a deprived former mining community. This will be achieved by drawing down appropriate grants from a variety of sources not available to public authorities. The project is empowering the community, will give local employment, and will yield over 60% reduction in current CO_2 emissions to atmosphere.*

Contractors might be able to offer cheaper or better alternatives either at the outset or as a consequence of new product or system developments. The former situation is best resolved by:

- consulting potential suppliers and contractors on the proposed specification before seeking tenders
- allowing contractors to offer alternatives in their bids. But, in order to allow fair comparison with other offers, the original specification must be priced. Contractors who wish to do so can then offer their alternatives, demonstrating how these would modify their tender.

The problem of ensuring that acceptable changes can be incorporated into a contract during its tenancy needs careful resolution. Supremely, changes should benefit the recipients of the service. The Contractor's proposal for any change should be in writing and be accompanied by a clear analysis of the reasons for the proposed change and the benefits and cost differences compared with the original specification.

Financial commitment

We have commented already on the need to ensure the Authority can continue to meet its financial commitments, especially of Term Contracts. For several years Authorities have been advised to adopt financial systems which clearly show commitments. The nature of annual budgeting and the variable value of Term Contract payments militate against simplicity. Even so, Authorities are well advised to grapple with and seek resolutions to the issues. Account managers cannot make proper management decisions without comprehensive financial information. The level of commitment is an essential element of that.

Statutes

Contracts are inevitably subject to the law of contract. But recent years have seen more primary legislation regulating the relationship between parties to a contract. Statute takes precedence over agreements made between parties to a contract. There are exceptions where statute allows parties to regulate their relationship in a manner effectively enhancing that required by statute. The contract writing bodies listed in Appendix A issue amendments to their standard contracts as new legislation is enacted. Elsewhere we advise use of standard contracts whenever possible. Authorities who write their own contracts or adapt standard ones for their own use should take great care to ensure that all current legislation has been incorporated.

Audit support

Auditors play an important role in the procurement process, including:

- checks to ensure the proper procedures have been followed
- checks to ensure that the contractor is paid the appropriate amount, especially the final sum due under the contract
- investigations of any alleged improper behaviour.

Auditors should not become involved in the procurement process itself, nor in the supervision or monitoring of contractors. The greatest value of Audit is their impartiality and rigour of their investigations. However, the Audit process can be helped greatly by the nature and accuracy of the records kept. Any review of or change to established procurement strategies should seek advice from Auditors to ensure that:

- probity is safeguarded
- procedures are clear and understandable
- responsibilities for decision making are allocated to named individuals or specific committees
- appropriate records of all tendering and contract transactions are maintained in such a way as to facilitate audit.

Innovation and risk

We live in a developing world. New technologies, new systems and new materials combine with a changing environment and rising aspirations. However novel a contract specification might be at its inception, ideally it should still be capable of accommodating change. There are three possible approaches:

- keep contracts, especially Term Contracts, to short durations and revise the specification before re-tendering
- incorporate changes into the contract once the new technology or new requirement is fully understood and specified
- encourage the contractor to seek innovative measures in anticipation of possible changes.

The first involves no risk, but may deprive the recipients of the service of the potential benefits of developing technology. The second, measured, approach may ensure that the service does not fall too far behind the best, but it is still unlikely to achieve the continuous improvements and excellence expected by Best Value. Encouraging innovation is the most risky but potentially the most beneficial course. Clearly the contract cannot anticipate what innovations might be adopted during its tenancy, but the allocation of risk and the sharing of any benefits can be set out. Known as 'pain/gain share', the contract should provide a framework for agreeing on the implementation of beneficial innovations and the sharing of the costs and savings resulting from their introduction. Innovation should not be haphazard. Each proposition should be subject to an appraisal agreed between the parties to the contract. In this context, partnering is the ideal vehicle for innovation.

Public support

Authorities create 'public goods' – those facilities and services provided for the community as a whole. Welfare economics recognizes that, in a developed community, any worthwhile change will deliver benefits to many but also impose costs (or disbenefits) on some. Whilst some investment is essential and unarguable (such as the provision of sewers for public health) much of what Authorities do affects the quality of life of individuals. The commercial sector widely acknowledges the importance of market research and public relations. Authorities have been slow to incorporate market research as a fundamental basis for decision making. Yet innumerable techniques have been developed to assist people to articulate their needs and preferences. Authority contract specifications should be based on a clear understanding of the community's wishes and should ensure the public is kept informed of the service delivered by the contract. Elsewhere we argue the need to incorporate public response in service and hence in contract reviews. Inevitably the procurement strategy is closely allied to the authority's public consultation/involvement strategy.

Misunderstandings

Misunderstandings can and do happen. However well intentioned, a Contractor under pressure, especially if the Contractor's margins are slim, may omit or truncate some aspect of the service delivery. Similarly, the instructions issued on behalf of the authority might be somewhat ambiguous. In the final analysis, the misunderstanding can become a dispute whose resolution will require a formal system (see Chapter 17).

The procurement strategy and its implementation should seek to minimize the probability of misunderstanding between the parties to a contract. There are several steps that you can take:

- Ensure the specification is clear. Have it checked by an experienced person not involved in the initial drafting.
- Use standard contract documents and hence well-tried and familiar contract procedures.
- Ensure the Authority's supervising officer and the main contractor's agent are compatible and are agreed on their objectives and working systems. Such compatibility and agreement are fundamental to part-nering (see Chapter 8).
- Establish quick and effective communication to raise issues and confirm instructions.
- Review progress and invite comment on the contract.
- Ensure service recipients are kept informed and that their expectations are being met.
- Ensure fair and timely payments.

Payments

Cash flow is crucial to a business. Authority staffs do not experience the problems of adverse cash flow, since the Authority receives much of its income in advance of providing the services. Late and non-payment is the largest single cause of business bankruptcy. Whilst recent legislation requires that contractors be paid to a pre-determined time-scale, those who do not receive payments in full or to time are reluctant to take action to recover their dues for fear of adversely affecting their chances of winning further work from the Authority. Many reasons have been cited for late payment, from over-zealous accountants to lost post or system breakdowns. Whilst such reasons may be true, they confirm that the Authority is failing in its duty. The contractor should not be the loser. In truth, the reputations of such Authorities result in higher tender prices to cover unreliable payment. Best Value, legislation and the contract conditions require consis-tent, fair and timely payment of contractors. The procurement system review should be accompanied by a review of the Authority's creditor system.

Client competence

Whether the Authority procures its services through a traditional route or by partnering, the results depend on the quality and experience of the people involved. Some Authorities would appear to believe that only the contractor needs quality staff. This is demonstrably not so. The Authority that seeks to deliver Best Value should be represented by equally competent staff. Competence comes through:

- *Appropriate educational/professional base.* In particular, the individual should be able to think through the problems of service delivery and be able to find appropriate solutions.

- *Experience*. The Authority will benefit from individuals with not only experience of similar services or contracts but also the ability to communicate and negotiate effectively.
- *Training*. Training is work-directed learning. On-going training (or 'continuous professional development') is a requirement of most professional staff. In this context staff will need training in the procurement processes, ramifications of the forms of contract used by the Authority and, in particular, any new approaches such as partnering.

Sub-contracting

The construction industry, in particular, operates on the basis that sub-contractors undertake much of the work. Whether or not this is right, the fact must be acknowledged. It is impractical to forbid the use of sub-contractors. Indeed, it can be argued that contractors have a right to employ appropriate sub-contractors. By the same token, the employing Authority should also have the right to object, on reasonable grounds, to the use of specific sub-contractors. The recent revision of the ICE standard 'Measurement Contract' seeks to reconcile these potentially conflicting rights. The main Contractor is well advised, in any case, to select sub-contractors with care and to advise the Authority accordingly. Sub-contractors should be expected to comply with all the contract conditions set out in the main contract with the Authority, especially those matters relating to Health and Safety and care for the public.

Some Authorities use the facility of nominating sub-contractors for particular elements of the service. There is a risk in this course of action. The main Contractor may be able to select a sub-contractor better able to perform the tasks and with whom a partnering relationship has been established already. Unless there is an absolute necessity, such as lead times extending before the appointment of the main Contractor, prior nomination of sub-contractors may well not yield Best Value.

Review

We have emphasized that review is an indispensable part of good management. The procurement strategy should be reviewed; indeed, this is the subject of this publication. But so also should key elements of the processes be reviewed. In our experience, most would agree their importance, but few undertake structured reviews of Authority practices. Review should be a structured and a disciplined process. The purpose of review is not to lay blame for errors or deficiencies in performance, but to understand contractual processes better, so enabling improvements to be defined.

Various formal techniques have been developed. One such utilizes brainstorming to list 'what went well' and 'what went badly' so as to form an agenda for deciding on 'what to do differently next time'. Key to the success of review are:

- a positive approach
- the involvement of all those directly involved
- inclusion of representatives of recipients of the service (the customers)
- an understood review method
- implementation of review recommendations.

Best Value seeks continuous improvement. Regular, timetabled reviews are a key driver of real improvements.

Health and safety

Despite legislation, the safety record, especially in the construction industry, is poor and has not improved. This is unacceptable. Public Authorities should set exemplary standards of care for those it employs, whether directly or through contractors. The Health and Safety Act was enacted in 1974, so Authorities and their employees should be familiar with their responsibilities. The more recent Regulations covering Construction and Design place further duties on the Authority, its designers and constructors. The procurement strategy should confirm rigorous compliance with Health and Safety regulations. Indeed, Health and Safety policies may well need to be reviewed in association with the procurement strategy.

From incidental surveys, it would appear that the main hindrance to safe working is cost cutting. Authorities should ensure that no such accusation could be made of the way they manage. Similarly, tenderers should be asked to confirm both the content of their Health and Safety policy and also their commitment to the fulfilling of their stated aims. Specifications could well list those matters where safety risk analysis should be carried out and where Performance Statements of safe working practice are required. Nevertheless, Contractors should be advised to undertake their own hazard identification and institute appropriate safe working procedures.

Safety does not start when a contract is let. Safety should be inherent in all decision making, from identifying people's needs (Step 1 in Chapter 2) and in every step of the procurement process right through to the review of achievements.

16 Monitoring

Effective monitoring is essential for defining and securing continuous improvements. Monitoring is undertaken at three distinct levels:

- To assess the existing position. Sometimes known as 'situational analysis', surveys and checks confirm the current position. The information required may include the physical condition of assets, their usage and people's needs and aspirations, as well as their opinions of the current situation, the immediate environment, and the impact on other activities or policies.
- To check whether the service performance is meeting the requirements. In what way is the service changing the existing situation? This level of monitoring should include the physical changes, resources used and the effects on recipients and the environment. Market research that checks people's reactions and opinions should be a feature.
- To check that the contractor is meeting the contract specification. There are various ways to check contract performance including direct supervision, periodic measurement and audit.

Monitoring is most effective if:

- Clear measurements can be used. Progress should be quantified whenever possible. Qualitative assessment tends to rely on opinion and judgement and is thereby a less reliable guide.
- It compares actual with expected performance. Monitoring needs a base for comparison. Whilst comparison can be made with the original assessment of the 'existing situation', by definition the 'existing' is an historic snapshot. So a key element of business (or service) planning is to forecast expected performance. The more detailed the forecasts, the clearer should be the monitoring.

The purpose of monitoring is to ensure decisions are based on relevant factual information. Monitoring of a service or a specific contract should inform management decisions that yield the best possible outcome. Monitoring involves measurement. In itself, it uses resources. Careful planning is essential to ensure the greatest degree of economy, yet producing effective information. Generally key parameters will be defined and used in the comparisons between actual and forecast performance. Knowledge of statistical techniques, especially of sampling theory, will ensure only the necessary quantity of data is collected and analysed.

Traditional contracts have taken great care in specifying the inputs required to produce the required asset or service. Both the standard of the materials and the performance of individual activities have been specified. This type of contract generally rewards the contractor on the basis of actual measured quantities of work done to specification. The Client can be assured that the outcome meets original intentions, but monitoring inevitably involves checking the contractors 'workmanship', materials used and quantities. This 'supervision' requires that the Client's monitoring staffs are knowledgeable, experienced and fair in their judgements. There is a cost associated with this level of monitoring, but the client can be assured of compliance with the contract.

Chapters 6 and 7 compare different forms of contract that are available now, whilst Chapter 8 discusses the use of a Partnering approach. Each form of contract allocates risks in a particular manner. The level and type of monitoring will vary. As part of any Procurement Strategy review, Authorities should reconsider the types of contract they use. In making their decision, Authorities should take into account the type of monitoring necessary.

Whilst pre-selection of contractors should enable the Authority to invite only contractors with a proven track record, even the best contractor can make mistakes or misinterpret the Authority's wishes. The Authority should nominate an experienced individual (either from their own staff or from a third party) to supervise and monitor the contract performance in an appropriate and cost-effective manner.

Partnering implies that the Contractor will work with the Authority to ensure the contract is performed in the most economical but effective manner. The Authority should be able to trust the contractor to undertake all the agreed activities, so 'supervision' can be minimal or even eliminated. The Contractor will be paid from public resources, so performance must still be verified. Alternative approaches include:

- the collation by the Contractor of key statistics
- 'open book', whereby the Contractor's own records are made available to the client
- independent audit.

The Authority may reasonably expect the contractor to confirm consistency in the standards achieved by adhering to a Quality Assurance system.

Modern information technology offers opportunities for the collection and analysis of considerable volumes of data. Investment in systems can yield real savings in terms of speed of data processing and instant control of processes. Wastage and costs can be reduced. The procurement strategy should include appropriate systems to enable both the performance of the immediate contract to be monitored and also the wider effects to be assessed. Examples abound, and include remote monitoring of traffic flows and heating/ventilating plants. Investment in such systems should be justified by benefit–cost analysis.

The Audit Commission has devised a number of Performance Indicators. Whilst each is the result of extensive consultation, they all have natural limitations. At best, performance indicators enable checks on the key characteristics of a service. They do not allow for local variations, nor do they fully describe any service. Whilst useful as prime indicators, they must be supplemented with other performance measures. Indeed, the Best Value regime anticipates that Authorities will supplement the National Indicators with appropriate local ones. The applicability of indicators should itself be monitored. Indicators have a shelf life. New indicators should be introduced if they better reflect the purpose of the service. The underlying principle of monitoring remains that of securing Best Value to the Authority, but supremely for its customers.

Monitoring is not merely checking on others' performance. It is fundamental to a learning organization that they:

- discover how services can be delivered best
- find out what works well and what does not
- ensure that service recipients' needs are being met
- detect changes in needs and the delivery environment.

Authorities are then better placed to not only respond to the immediate situation, but also to plan the future with assurance.

National Indicator example

BV Code	Indicator	Target	Definition
BV105	Damage to roads and pavements	Local	Total number of all reported incidents of dangerous damage to roads and pavements repaired or made safe within 24 hours from the time that the authority first became aware of the damage, as a percentage of such incidents

Local Indicator example

Authority type	Indicator
Unitary	% of non-urgent highways repairs agreed to, completed within 28 days

17   Dispute resolution

Introduction

Before any contract is entered into it is necessary to consider the most appropriate manner in which disputes arising out of the contract are to be resolved.

If no provision is made in the contract itself the parties always have the right to apply to the courts, but this may not be the most appropriate or the most cost-effective means of resolving disputes likely to arise from a specialist contract.

There is a wide range of procedures available and in use by the construction industry. These include:

- expert determination
- mediation and conciliation
- adjudication
- arbitration
- litigation.

Each has it own advantages and disadvantages, and a knowledge of each of these procedures is essential so that a considered choice can be made.

Expert determination

Expert determination is a process whereby the parties agree to refer their dispute to an expert and agree to abide by the expert's decision. There is no appeal from an expert's decision. Right or wrong, it is enforceable[1] unless the expert answers the wrong question or goes outside his or her terms of reference.

Expert determination is useful and appropriate where the dispute concerns a particular field of expertise, such as the valuation of variations, determining a reasonable value, the interpretation of technical specification, or

---

1   Nikko Hotels (UK) Ltd *vs.* MEPC (1991) 2 EGLR 103.

assessing the reasonableness of an action taken by a person acting in a technical capacity.

Expert determination is used extensively for rent reviews, but its use in the construction industry is limited in standard contracts. The main user is the Institution of Chemical Engineers, who incorporate it for disputes concerning the valuation of variations.[2]

Mediation and conciliation

Mediation and conciliation are both processes whereby an independent person, a neutral, attempts to broker a settlement between the parties by shuttle diplomacy. It is a voluntary process, and its advocates maintain that it is only effective if the parties embark upon it willingly for each dispute that arises.

A mediator has no power of determination, and if an agreement is not reached the process comes to an end and some other procedure must then be invoked.

In the construction industry few of the standard contracts include provision for mediation. Exceptions are FIDIC,[3] which are used for international contracts, and the ICE Conditions, which are used for UK civil engineering works. Under the FIDIC contracts there is an arrangement for amicable settlement, and under the ICE Conditions there is a procedure called Conciliation.

The ICE Conciliation is conducted under the ICE Conciliation Procedure (1999),[4] and is a two-stage process. The first stage is mediation, during which the conciliator attempts to guide the parties to a settlement and, in default of a settlement, the second stage is a recommendation by the conciliator as to how the matter should be resolved. The recommendation is the conciliator's view and need not be based on any principles of contract or law. This is because the conciliator will, during the first stage, obtain confidential information from the parties, which may not be known to the other side. The recommendation becomes final and binding upon the parties if neither party issues a notice, within a month of receiving the recommendation, to refer the dispute to arbitration.

Experience shows that most disputes either settle at the conciliation meeting or as a result of negotiations based on the recommendation.

---

2   *Model forms of Conditions of Contract for Process Plant – Lump Sum and Reimbursable Contracts*, IChemE, Davis Building, 165–189 Railway Terrace, Rugby CV21 3HQ.
3   Fédération Internationale des Ingénieurs-Conseils, PO Box 86, CH 1000 Lausanne 12, Switzerland.
4   A copy can be obtained from the bookshop, the Institution of Civil Engineers, 1 Great George Street, London SW1P 3AA.

Adjudication

Until recently,[5] adjudication was not governed by any statute but was a private arrangement by which the parties agreed to empower an individual with the Authority to settle a dispute between them. This might be a very specific type of dispute[6] or a wide range of potential disputes. It was essentially a form of expert determination, but where the decision was to be binding it has been held to be an agreement to arbitrate.[7] The legal position was therefore uncertain.

Recent legislation has introduced adjudication as the normal form of dispute resolution for construction contracts,[8] which include the design of, carrying out of and giving advice on construction operations. The Act gives the parties the right to an adjudication procedure complying with the Act. The Act sets out eight principles,[9] which if incorporated into the contract provide a procedure that satisfies its requirements. If these eight principles are not incorporated into the contract then the right is exercisable in accordance with a procedure set out in the Scheme for Construction Contracts Regulations 1998.[10]

Statutory adjudication is basically a 28 day procedure, although this period can be extended with the agreement of the parties. It was introduced to aid cash flow and to prevent disputes from delaying the construction work. It is therefore quick and relatively cheap.

There is no need to take any action to include adjudication in a construction contract, but it is necessary to include the name of an appointing body for the adjudicator in case the parties cannot agree a name. If the Scheme is used then the party initiating the adjudication can apply to an Adjudicator Nominating body, which is defined in the Act as any 'body (not being a natural person and not being a party to the dispute) which holds itself out publicly as a body which will select an adjudicator when requested to do so by a referring party'.[11] This could prove unacceptable to a responding party if an inappropriate body is chosen.

However, the Scheme is embryonic and contains a number of issues that may be unsatisfactory to parties. A number of bodies publish adjudication procedures which are said to comply with the Act and which are tailored to particular branches of the industry. These procedures clarify certain areas of doubt found in the Scheme and clarify the manner in which the adjudication is to be conducted. Among the most popular procedures are the procedures published by The Institution of Civil Engineers, the Construction

---

5   The Housing Grants, Construction & Regeneration Act 1996 [HGC&R Act 1996].
6   For instance, the contractor's right to set off under DOM/1 conditions.
7   Cape Durasteel Limted *vs.* Rosser & Russell Building Services Limited [(1995) 46 Cons LR 75].
8   See ss 104 and 105 of HGC&R Act 1996.
9   See s 108 of HGC&R Act 1996.
10 There are separate versions, but largely similar, for England and Wales, Scotland and Northern Ireland.
11 Paragraph 2(3) of The Scheme for Construction Contracts (England and Wales) Regulations 1998.

Industry Council and the Technology and Construction Courts Solicitors' Association (TeCSA). Consideration should be given to incorporating one of these procedures into any construction contract that does not incorporate one of the Standard Forms.

The adjudicator's decision is summarily enforceable in the courts and is temporarily binding upon the parties until the dispute is finally settled by litigation or arbitration.[12] This is a radical change because it means that any money decided to be payable by an adjudicator is paid immediately and is not held up until the matter is finally determined, by the House of Lords if necessary, as is the case with litigation.

Arbitration

Arbitration is private and can be invoked only by agreement between the parties, generally by incorporation into the contract. Arbitration is generally governed by statute[13] and is subject to general control by the courts. An arbitrator's award is enforceable summarily in the courts of most countries[14] and is therefore advisable for international contracts.

The arbitrator is chosen for his or her expertise in the subject matter of the dispute and will not generally be a lawyer. Arbitration is conducted in private and is confidential. No one other than those involved is entitled to attend a hearing. The arbitrator's award may itself be confidential unless it is subject to appeal in the courts.

The arbitrator's jurisdiction (that is, what the arbitrator can decide) is governed by the arbitration agreement, which is generally the dispute resolution clause contained in the contract. Where a standard form, such as the ICE Conditions of Contract (7th Edition) is incorporated into the contract by reference, it is advisable that the words 'including the arbitration clause' be included in the reference because difficulties have been experienced where this has not been done.[15]

To incorporate arbitration into a contract there are two essential requirements. First, the arbitration agreement itself, which will generally be in the form:

> Should any dispute or difference arise between the parties in connection with or arising out of the contract it shall be referred to the arbitration of

---

12 S 108 (3) of HGC&R Act 1996.

13 Arbitration Act 1996 in England and Wales and Northern Ireland. There is no statute for Scotland and Scots law of arbitration has been established by precedent.

14 All those that are signatories to the *Convention on the Recognition and Enforcement of Foreign Arbitral Awards* adopted by the United Nations Conference on International Commercial Arbitration on 10 June 1958.

15 Aughton Ltd *vs.* MF Kent Services Ltd [57BLR 1], Black Country Development Corporation *vs.* Kier Construction Limited [80 BLR 102].

a single arbitrator agreed by the parties or in default of agreement a person appointed by [the nominating body named in the contract].

The second requirement is to name an appointing body for the arbitrator should the parties be unable to agree the name of a person. The major technical institutions,[16] the Law Society and the Chartered Institute of Arbitrators all provide this service.

The right of appeal from an arbitrator's award is very limited. There is no right of appeal on a finding of fact and a limited right concerning points of law. An arbitrator's award is therefore more likely to be final than that of a judge at first instance.

Litigation

Litigation, which means resolution by the courts, is available to everyone unless they expressly contract out of it. This can be done expressly by a clause in the contract or impliedly by including an arbitration clause.

For small claims,[17] application can be made to the small claims courts, which apply an arbitral procedure for hearing the evidence. This is cheap and relatively quick, but enforcement can be difficult.

For larger disputes, application is made either to the County Court, for claims under £50 000, or otherwise the High Court. Court proceedings can be both expensive and lengthy. The dispute is settled by a judge, who is versed in the law but not necessarily the subject matter of the dispute. It is for this reason that other forms of dispute resolution are often advocated.

Decisions of the lower courts are subject to appeal on both the facts and the law, which may delay settlement for a considerable time.

Conclusions

A wide range of dispute resolution procedures is available for contracts in the construction industry, and the choice of procedure should be given thought before the contract is let.

Adjudication is now generally available except for supply contracts, but care should be taken to ensure that an appropriate nominating body for the adjudicator is agreed in the contract. You should decide whether to specify one of the standard procedures or rely upon the Scheme for Construction Contracts.

---

16 Institution of Civil Engineers (ICE), the Royal Institute of British Architects (RIBA) and the Royal Institution of Chartered Surveyors (RICS).
17 Currently £3000.

Arbitration for construction disputes is generally preferable to litigation because of its confidential nature and the technical nature of most disputes.

Consideration should be given to expert determination for supply-only contracts and issues concerning valuations.

If no special provisions are made, disputes will be settled in the courts.

18 Conclusions

Procurement is complex, both in the variety of services needed and the choice of techniques available. As more services are acquired, so the opportunities to realize substantial benefits for the Authority multiply. Conversely, poorly specified and ill-considered purchases will lead to low-quality and unnecessarily expensive services. Procurement is not in itself a difficult process to understand, but there is a logical sequence and there are many opportunities for modernizing and improvement.

The main cause of 'failures' in procurement stem from ill-considered or inadequate briefs. Successful procurement starts with clarity of thought and precise articulation of what is needed. Need is not the sole province of the elected member or professional officer. It can only be deduced by proper investigation of those people in the community who are the intended recipients of services. Once those needs are understood, members and officers should bring their expertise to define a vision of a better future and find the most economical way to achieve that vision.

Best Value is about the manner in which services are defined and delivered. The underlying assumption is that Authorities could and should do better than they are. There is ample evidence to support this assumption. Authorities have a duty to review all their services in order to determine their current performance and more particularly how they can improve. Best Value is not a criticism. It is a methodology for incorporating in public services the best of commercial sector practices. It is a challenge that Authorities dare not ignore.

Management theorists have long advocated the necessity of continuous improvement if a business is to survive. Best Value imports that necessity into Authorities. Some have been practising the theory; others have considerable ground to catch up. So Government has signalled the need to preface continuous improvement by a step change. The first stage in step change is not to examine individual services but to review the overall working of the Authority. Of prime importance is its procurement strategy.

Our experience, supported by incidental surveys, confirms the conservative nature of many Authorities. We know of one still using a form of contract superseded over 30 years ago. Not only have techniques changed, but also the very nature of service provision is more exacting. Over the past few years, Government has enacted several statutes that impinge directly on the relationships between client and contractor. Similarly, the EC continues to be concerned with their objective of better competition between service providers and are drafting further Directives to achieve their aims. Whilst we would advocate that no more legislation is added until proven necessary, many Authorities have yet to realize the impact of recent legislation and implement its requirements. We believe that all Authorities must give a high priority to reviewing and improving their knowledge of the rules governing procurement.

Procurement strategy review does not mean the invention of new forms of contractual relationship. Risk is a key determinant in the price charged by a contractor. It is far better to use standard forms of contract understood by all parties. Should Authorities believe that these standard forms lack some essential element, they are well able to instigate review and improvement either directly with the contract-writing body or through their representative members of the body.

We are concerned by the erroneous notion that contractors are best placed to provide all of an Authority's services, including advice to members. Contractors might be the most efficient means of providing specific services, once they have been properly specified. The acid test is competition. But to expect unbiased advice from a contractor is naive. The Authority will continue to need experienced and exceptionally well-trained advisors. The core advisory service is best provided by directly employed staff, but with access to specialists drawn from other sectors.

Procurement is a learning process. As services are implemented, so the reactions of users will inform and guide refinements to the service. The process itself presents opportunities to gain insights into commercial practice, legal interpretation and individual relationships. The wise Authority learns from these experiences and refines its own practices.

In whatever state your Authority might be, there is ample scope to benefit the community you serve by improving your procurement strategy. All you need is good leadership, a clear vision and the determination to succeed.

Appendix A
Forms of contract available

NEC – New Engineering Contract
- ECC Option A Activity schedule
- ECC Option B Quantitive
- ECC Option C Target Cost Activity schedule
- ECC Option D Target Cost – Quantitative
- ECC Option E Cost reimbursable
- ECC Option F Management Contract
- The Engineering and Construction Short Contract (ECSC)
- The Engineering and Construction Sub-contract
- The Professional Services Contract
- The Adjudicators Contract
- The Engineering and Construction Short Sub-contract

ICE Conditions of Contract, and associated contracts
- 5th Edition
- CECA Subcontract to 5th Edition
- 6th Edition
- CECA Subcontract to 6th Edition
- 7th Edition
- CECA Subcontract to 7th Edition
- Minor Works 3rd Edition
- Design and Construct 2nd Edition
- CECA Subcontract to Design and Construct
- Ground Investigation
- Agreement for Consultancy Work in Respect of Domestic or Small Works
- ACE Conditions of Engagement
- A (1) Lead Consultant
- A (2) Lead Consultant (M & E)
- B (1) Consultant
- B (2) Consultant (M & E)
- C (1) Consultant to D & C Contractor
- D Report & Advisory

JCT – Joint Contracts Tribunal
- Standard From (JCT)
- Subcontract (NSC)
- Subcontract DOM/1
- Prime Cost Contract (PCC)
- PCC Subcontract
- Contractors Design (CD)
- Subcontract DOM/2
- Management Contract (MC)
- Works Contract
- Intermediate Form Contract (IFC)
- Subcontract (IN/SC)
- Minor Works (MW)
- Measured Term Contract (MTC)
- Home owner

FIDIC – Fédération International Des Ingénieurs Conseils
- Red Book Old
- Orange Book
- FIDIC Silver 1998
- FIDIC Yellow 1998
- FIDIC Red 1998
- FIDIC Green 1998

GC/Works – General Conditions/Works
- GC Works 1
- GC Works 2
- GC Works 1998 (PACE)

IChemE – Institution of Chemical Engineers
- Red Book (Lump sum)
- Green Book (Cost reimbursable)

Water Industry
- MF/1
- G90

Conditions of engagement
ACA
- ACA
- PPC 2000

RIBA – Royal Institute of British Architects

Petrochemical industry
- Cost Reduction in the New Era (CRINE)

MOD – Ministry of Defence
- DEFCON 2000

Bespoke

Procurement Forms of Contract can vary widely with a significant number of options available. The list may be divided by the following categories:

- Goods
- Professional services
- Works

Each of these can be procured by a variety of generic approaches:

- Purchase orders
- Work orders
- Exchange of letters
- Formal one-off contracts
- Term contracts/agreements
- Partnering arrangements
- Design and build
- Lump sum
- Target cost
- Fixed price

Appendix B
Other legislative requirements

PFI Regulations: Initially brought into effect on 31 October 1996 by the Local Authorities (Capital Finance) (Amendment No. 3) Regulations 1996 (S12539). Amendments were made in the course of incorporating the regulations into the Local Authorities (Capital Finance) Regulations 1997 (S1319).

Further, mainly clarifying, amendments were introduced by the Local Authorities (Capital Finance) (Amendment) Regulations 1998 (s1371), which came into force on 20 March 1998.

The Local Government (Contracts) Act 1997: introduced in recognition of the growing uncertainty about Authority power to contract with the Private Sector for the provision of assets and services, and of the likelihood that this would impede the development of public-private partnership schemes.

The Local Government (Contracts) Act 1997 is a measure to encourage and enable Local Authorities to explore the scope for partnerships with the Private Sector.

Equalities: Contractors shall be required to provide answers to the approved questions concerning equality, and provide documentary evidence as allowed under the Local Government Act 1988.

The TUPE situation is still developing and a definitive paragraph will be added in due course, however the current situation is that although revision has been made to the Acquired Rights Directive, draft Regulations to implement the revised Directive are still awaited from the DTI. Implementation of the Directive needs to take place by Spring 2001. The definition of transfer of an undertaking is also in question, for example when TUPE should and should not apply.

Health and Safety at Work etc. Act 1974

Construction (Design and Management) Regulations 1994